Aaron French

Notes on the surnames of Francus, Farnceis, French, etc. in Scotland

With an account of the Frenches of Thorndykes

Aaron French

Notes on the surnames of Francus, Farnceis, French, etc. in Scotland
With an account of the Frenches of Thorndykes

ISBN/EAN: 9783337281427

Printed in Europe, USA, Canada, Australia, Japan

Cover: Foto ©Andreas Hilbeck / pixelio.de

More available books at **www.hansebooks.com**

NOTES

SURNAMES OF FRANCUS, FRANCEIS, FRENCH, Etc., IN
SCOTLAND, WITH AN ACCOUNT OF THE
FRENCHES OF THORNYDYKES

BY

A. D. WELD FRENCH

*Author of the " Index Armorial," Fellow of the Society of Antiquaries of Scotland, Member
of the Scottish History Society and of the Committee on Heraldry of the
New England Historic Genealogical Society*

BOSTON
PRIVATELY PRINTED
1893

PREFACE.

THE authorities consulted in this work were the abbey records, the principal antiquarian authorities, and published and unpublished public records.

In regard to the early use of these surnames in France and Scotland, some remarks seem appropriate in this place. From the Latin word " Francus," with the addition of the suffixes, we have the following compound words,—" Franc-ensis," " Franc-iscus," and " Franci-gena."

The change of Francensis to the modern Les Français is not only interesting as regards the changes of a word in the language of France, but also of some value as bearing on the commencement and continued use of these surnames.

The suffix *ensis* in Franc-ensis implies nationality in Latin; and we observe, according to M. Brachet, that by reducing the *ns* to *s* we have Francēsis, then Francisis in the seventh century, Francéis in the tenth century, at its end *éi* becomes *ói*, and we have

Françóis, by the end of the twelfth century *ói* becomes *óe;* and we have Françóes, then Françoés and
Les Français.

We have also from Francus the French surnames
of Le Franc and Le Franceis; * and at later periods,
owing to the changes in the orthography of the language, Le François and finally Le Français came
into existence.

The surname of Le Franc is more frequently found
in France, but it does not often occur in the records
of Great Britain. Its nearest approach, of which
there are numerous records, are *Franc̄* or *Le Franc̄.*
This mark of abbreviation indicates a contraction for
Francus or Le Franceis.

Surnames came into existence in France toward
the end of the tenth century. In the following century are found the names of Gualterius Francus and
Hugo Franco. About the middle of the twelfth century the records of the Cotentin show the names of
Rannulfus Francus and Ricardo Franco.

---

* This name passed through many orthographical changes in
Great Britain before the anglicization period. In Scotland the
Coldingham charters, of which abstracts are hereafter given, show
sufficient illustrations, of which the following may be mentioned;
namely, Franceis, Fraunceis, Franceys, Fraunceys, etc. Some
illustrations of the early anglicized surname of French in Scotland
are found in the latter part of the fifteenth and earlier portion of
the sixteenth century in the records relating to the family of
Johannes France, Burgess of Linlithgow, where it appears in the
year 1487 under the form of France, in the year 1535 as Frans,
Franss, and Franche, while under the date of 1538-39 this surname
is found first in this family under the form of Frensch.

M. Pinckmeier and M. Bain translate Franciscus as French. Their opinions have the confirmation of M. Du Cange, who gives the following illustrations, "Franciscus habitus, Cuspis Franciscus, Miles Franciscus, Franciscus mos, and Francisca lingua."

From Franciscus we have Francisco, which we find synonymous with Le Franceis in the Coldingham charters. In one of the charters of Robert de Brus, circa 1218, we find William Franceis; and at the same period, in another of his charters, apparently the same individual has his surname latinized into Willielmus Franciscus.

As regards Francigena and Franceis being synonymous, we have the record of the parson of Coldebec, in Cumberland, who is mentioned in 1231–33 as John Francigena, and again in this same period as John Le Franceis. M. Stapleton evidently took this view, as his French translation of Walterus Francigena, who is mentioned in the Norman Roll of 1203, was Walter Le Franceis; while Roger French is given by the Rev. Eyton as the English translation of Rogerus Francigena, who is mentioned in England in the early part of the thirteenth century.

There remains now the pleasant duty of thanking those who have aided in this work, without whose co-operation and help it could not have been completed. My obligations are due to Dr. Thomas Dickson, Curator of the Historical Department H. M. General Register House at Edinburgh, who, on learning of my wish, kindly placed at my disposal for examination his valuable unpublished records; and I must specially acknowledge the interest he showed in the work during its progress. To my friend, Rev. Walter MacLeod, the antiquary, I must express my gratitude for his interest, perseverance, care, and the most satisfactory results of his examinations of the archives and manuscripts of Scotland. With the Norman charters, of which translations are given, my special thanks are due M. François Dolbet, the Registrar of the Archives of La Manche, at Saint-Lo, France, who, on being informed of my desire to have the abbey manuscript records of La Manche examined, kindly offered to make a search among these ancient archives. With great antiquarian zeal he completed the examination of these records from their foundations down to the time that King John of England by his feudal delinquency lost the Duchy of Normandy. Some additional charters are given by him, showing the continuance of this surname in the Cotentin after its confiscation by King Philippe of France.

The remaining Norman charters presented were obtained from the published records. In conclusion I must acknowledge the thanks due Mr. George H. Ellis of this city for the typography of the work.

A. D. WELD FRENCH.

160 State Street, Boston, Mass., U.S.,
        December 15, 1893.

PART FIRST.

NOTES

ON THE SURNAMES OF FRANCUS, FRANCEIS, FRENCH IN SCOTLAND.

NOTES ON THE SURNAMES.

THE earliest vestiges in Scotland of the surname of French are found in the records of the old monasteries, as well as in ancient individual charters, where its prototypes will be observed under the forms of Francus, Franciscus, Francigena, Franceis, and Franke. These ancient surnames may be seen in the Chartularies of Coldingham, Coldstream, Cambuskeneth, Kelso, Melrose, and Newbottle; in the charters of Bruce, Normanville, and others. In my preface to the "Index Armorial" in the part relating to England, reference has been made to the Albeneios, Bruces, Foliots, and the Valoines, as originally coming from the Cotentin in Normandy. In Scotland you find the Morvilles and Franceis as well as the Bruces and Valoines, whose surnames all appear in the records of the Cotentin in the early part of the twelfth century.

The Bruces held Annandale in Scotland, the Morvilles held most of Lauderdale as well as large possessions in Teviotdale. These families, as well as the Valoines, were among the early benefactors to the Abbey of Melrose; while Hugh Morville was at least a very early benefactor of Dryburgh Abbey, if not the original founder.

The system of early colonization in Scotland is well illustrated by "the charter of Thor-longus, who settled there in the time of King Edgar. He had a grant of Ednaham, which was then a waste, and which he improved by his own money and people." Chalmer, referring to the system of English colonization in Scotland, "states that a baron obtained from the king a grant of lands which he settled with his followers, built a castle, a church, a mill, and a brewhouse, and thereby formed a hamlet, which in the practice of the age was called the Ton of the Baron." This, we judge, was not only the method of the English, but about the same system pursued by the Anglo-Norman colonists in the time of King David I.

We will now proceed to take up more specially the records in connection with Scotland and Normandy; and as a preliminary, owing to the feudality existing at a later period with the Bruces of Annandale, the record in connection with Robert de Brus of Yorkshire has more than usual significance. Reference is here made to a charter of Alanus de Percy, the son of Willielmus de Percy, which the Rev. J. C. Atkinson states was certainly executed between the years 1097 and 1101. In this document, as found in the manuscript of the Cartularum Abbathiæ de Whiteby at the British Museum, it will be observed that among the witnesses were "Robertus de Bruse et tres de suis militibus Rogerus de Rosels, Wydo de Lofthous et *Robertus ffraunceys.*" *

This is the *earliest record* the writer has thus far discovered of one of the name *of Fraunceys bearing a prænomen*, or baptismal name, in Great Britain, as well as the first instance thus far coming under his observation of one of this surname having feudal relations with the Bruces. Here we have a name first appearing about one-third of a century after the conquest of England, with feudal relations with the second Robert de Brus, who obtained possessions in Scotland, the son of one of the companions of William the Conqueror; and it is well authenticated that the surnames of Brus and Franceis were both identified with that part of the Cotentin of Normandy called the district of Valognes, in which was located Château d'Adam, the castle of Brix. Here, also, was the Abbey of Saint-Sauveur-le-Vicomte, which was so well endowed by the Bruces.

The Franceis were specially identified with the Abbey of Saint-Sauveur-le-Vicomte. Ranulphus Francus held land of this abbey; and *Ricardus Francus* once appears as a witness on behalf of the monks, and again as a witness to a charter in favor of this abbey.

---

* In the printed cartularum of this abbey the orthography of this surname was Français, hence the reason for its insertion in this latter form in the preface to my "Index Armorial" published in 1892.

Charter No. 1, that of *Rannulfus Francus*, is exceedingly interesting, as locating a family. By it it will be observed that he had sons, as well as a daughter of marriageable age, to whom he gives the land which he held in fee of this abbey. This seems to imply that he had other possessions of which the abbey were not overlords; and, as there is nothing thus far discovered to the contrary, it is inferred that he held his other possessions directly from King Stephen of England.

Mr. Dolbet fixes the date of this charter of *Rannulfus Francus* from 1147 to 1153, at which period Hugo was abbot.

The remaining charters to this and other abbeys of the Cotentin, where the surname of *Franceis* appears, are arranged by abbeys chronologically. Charters numbered two and three in favor of the Abbey of Saint-Sauveur were made by members of Anglo-Norman families who are particularly identified with what may be called the Valognes district of the Cotentin. The records confirm that the early *Franceis* of the Cotentin were from this district; and there is nothing in the Magni Rotuli Scaccarii Normanniæ to show that *Willielmus Franceis and Rogerus Franceis*, with records respectively of the years 1180 and 1195, were of any other location than this district, the latter Christian names, as already stated in the preface to my " Index Armorial," appearing in Scotland after the confiscation of Normandy, in 1204, by King Philippe II. of France. The charters numbered six, seven, eight, nine, ten, and eleven, found among the records of the Abbeys Cæsarisburgus and Montebourg, as well as the archives of the Abbey of Cerisy, specially show that this surname continued in the Valognes district of the Cotentin after the confiscation.

In charter No. 4 *Hugo Francus* is a witness, between the years 1113 and 1151, to a charter of Guido, Lord of Lavalle, to the monks of Savigny.

In the charter numbered six, in favor of the Abbey of Cherbourg, of the year 1234, will be found the name of *Willelmo Francesio, Canon of Cherbourg.*

Charters Nos. 8 and 9 are both identified with the viscounty of Valognes. The first of these charters is in favor of *Mathieu Le Franceis and Rose*, his wife. The other charter locates *Johan Le Franc as belonging to the parish of Cherbourg*, and mentions his *wife Juliane.*

Charter numbered ten is dated in the year 1316, and is found among the archives of the Abbey of Montebourg: in this *Michiel Le Franc* is the grantee of a piece of land in the parish of Saint Floissel.

The charter numbered eleven is that of *Alain Le François of the parish of Tessy*, in favor of the Abbey of Cerisy; and in it he mentions his *wife Thomasse.*

Charter No. 1.

Confirmation charter of the Abbey of Saint-Sauveur-le-Vicomte, to a charter of Rannulfus Francus, made between the years 1146 and 1154. To all persons, as well present as future. Know that *Rannulfus Francus*, with the consent of his sons, has granted to Gaufridus Britonus, with his daughter, as a marriage portion, the land he held of the abbey, reserving for said abbey one "mina" of grain; and the said Gaufridus shall hold it peacefully and freely, without any other service than giving the grain. This donation is granted, sealed, and confirmed by Abbot Hugo, with the consent of his chapter. Witnesses: Johannes, prior; Petrus, subprior; Willelmus, capellanus; Paganus, presbiterus; Rogerus de Hulmus; Robertus, son of Hamelinus; and many others.

Charter No. 2.

Charter of Robertus de Magnavilla * to the Abbey of Saint-Sauveur-le-Vicomte, circa 1136.

Robertus de Magnavilla and his wife Hadevisa and his son Radulfus grant to the Abbey of Saint Salvator ten acres of land in the ville of Radulfus (Rauville-le-Bigot in the arrondissement of Valognes), and "seipsos" after their death with everything they

---

* There is a commune of Mandeville in the arrondissement of Valognes in the Cotentin.

possessed. His witnesses: Radulfo Sueno, Osmundo de Brichebot, *Ricardo Franco*, and for the abbey's part Radulfo de Blihou and Ricardo, son of Radulfus.

Charter No. 3.

The donation of the church of Saint-Jean-des-Chênes by William de Vauville to Saint-Sauveur-le-Vicomte, circa 1155, namely,—

May it be known to all, as well present as future, that I, William de Vauville, have given to the Abbey of Saint-Sauveur the church of Saint-Jean-des-Chênes, which is situated in the Island of Jersey, with all tithes and rents belonging to same. I have also given to the said Abbey of Saint-Sauveur all that I had in the church of Saint Pierre de Fonteneio, near the ford, with all tithes and rents belonging to the same, with the consent of my wife and my sons, Richard and Leonc. Witnesses for my part: Ricardo, presbyter of Vauville; Roberto de Pert; Balduino, son of Adde; Philippo de Fonteneio; and, for the parts of the monks, Malgero de Fonteneio, *Ricardo Franco*, Petro, presbyter of Saint-Sauveur.

Charter No. 4.

Abbey of Savigny.

Charter of Guido de Lavalle to the donation of Gaudinus Rahier, M. Dolbet attributes this charter to Guy de Laval, who lived from 1113 to 1151.

To all the sons of Holy Mother Church, Guido, Lord of Lavalle, Greeting.

All of you know that Juhellus de Crapon, knight, granted to God and the monks of Savigny the land which Gaudinus Rahier had given them in perpetual alms, freely and quietly, and that the said monks therefor shall pay yearly 11 shillings (solidos Euronensium) on the day of Saint John the Baptist. Given in our presence, and in order that this charter may always remain irrefutable we have appended our seals. Witnesses: Willelmo de Clarisvallibus, Fulquerando de Altenosra, *Hugone Franco*, Gaufrido de Monte gaucheir, Guoslino de Cormeriis, Hugueto P., decano de Sabolio, et pluribus aliis.

Additional Charters, Nos. 5, 7, 8, and 9, of the Abbey of Cherbourg, from the work of M. Dubosc.

Charter No. 5.

Twelfth century. Sainte-Géneviève. Gatteville.

Charter of Amaury, son of Raoul. He grants to the canons of Notre-Dame-du-Vœu all his land of Guenestorp with house, and all the rents due him, with all the lands he possessed in the parish of Arreville and in the parish of Gatteville. The said donation is made for the welfare of the soul of Empress Matilde, of pious memory, and for the welfare of the soul of his father, mother, and ancestors. The

canons shall perpetually have in their society a canon
of his family, or another who may be designated, who
shall serve God in their house for his soul and those
of his ancestors. Witnesses: Petro, sacerdote de
Reiborne; Alexandro Canuto; Hugone, filio Richeri;
Willelmo Drubec; Roberto de Bosevilla; *Ricardo
Francesio;* Godefrido, filio sacerdotis.

Charter No. 6.

Abbey of Cherbourgh. A.D. 1234.

May it be known to all, as well present as future,
that I, Richard Des Moutiers (de Monasteriis), son of
Robert Des Moutiers, have assigned and transferred
to the Abbot and Convent of Cherbourg (Cæsaris
burgus) certain land in the parish of Saint Petrus de
Alumna, which is situated on the mountain near by
the place where the river descends from the hamlet of
Bosquelle (hamello Bosquelli) and the mill of Ketefri,
which land was measured out in the presence of
Ricardus de Kerquevilla, prior of La Taille, and
Willelmo Francesio, his companion, canons of the
said abbey, and in my presence with many others.
I have made this conveyance and assignation to the
said abbot and convent in exchange for certain land,
which they held by donations of my ancestors, situated on the bottom of the valley, near the said
mountain, which land the aforesaid abbot and convent on my petition exchanged with me for the pur-

pose of overflowing as a fishpond. But, if it should be found that the aforesaid exchanged land in the valley cannot be flooded with water, it shall be used for pasturage, and be common as well for me as those who hold land of the said abbot and convent, either divided or in whole. And I and my heirs warrant this exchange to the aforesaid abbot and convent in perpetuity; and, that the present charter may always remain irrefutable, I have appended my seal, anno Domini m°. cc°. xxx. quarto.

Charter No. 7.

Year 1252. Official charter of the archdeacon of Paris, making known that before him Richard de Cherbourg (Ricardus de Caroburgo), son of the *late Odon Le Franc*, has given in pure and perpetual alms to the abbey of Cherbourg all that he received as successor of his father and mother, the anniversary of which shall be held every year in the said abbey.

Charter No. 8.

Year 1298. Sainte-Géneviève.

Letter of the Viscount of Valognes, making known that before Vincent Surel, clerk of the said viscounty, was present Henri Godel, of the parish of Cantelouf, who acknowledged that he had sold to *Mathieu Le*

Franceis and Rose, his wife, and their heirs, " diz
sous de tornois " yearly rent at the feast of Sainte
Perronele, with a loaf of bread and a hen at Christmas, to be given as the homage from the hand of
Estyenne Quieret, besides two pieces of land situated in the parish of Sainte-Géneviève, the first
adjoining the land of Guillame Le Rous and the
manor which belonged to Nicole Durdenier. The
second is that of Cavées de Hotot, adjoining the
land of Unffrey Lengleis, the land of Guillame Le
Bel, extending to the land of Guillame Hubert and
the road to Barfleu. Price of this sale was " six livres
de tornois." Given in 1298, the Wednesday after the
feast of the Nativity of Sainte-Marie-Virge.

Charter No. 9.

Year 1309. Letter of Robert de Conflans, keeper
of the seal of the viscounty of Valognes, making
known that before Vincent Surel, clerk of the said
viscounty, were present *Johan Le Franc, of the parish
of Cherbourg* (Chieresbourc), and Juliane, his wife,
to whom he gave authority, as hereafter stated.
They acknowledged that of their own free will they
had exchanged, quitted, and delivered to the religious
persons, the abbot and convent of Notre-Dame-du
Vœu, near Cherbourg, a piece of land, situated in
the parish of Esqueudreville, near to Le Machon,

adjoining the land of the said convent, for a yearly rent * of a bushel of wheat, measure of Cherbourg, to be delivered at Saint Michiel, a loaf of bread valued at a denier and a hen at Christmas, to be paid yearly to the said couple by the hand of the granetarius of the said convent.

Charter No. 10.

Abbey of Montebourg.   Year 1316.

To all who see or hear this letter Jehan de Baudian-court, keeper of the seal of the Viscounty of Valognes, Greeting. Know that before Vincent Surel, sworn clerk of said viscounty, were present Richard de La Lande of the parish of Montebourg, and Perronele, his wife, to whom he gave authority as hereafter stated, they freely and without being constrained having sold, quitted, and transferred to *Michiel Le Franc* all their right to a piece of land situated in the parish of Saint Floissel, near the bridge of Colin du Marest, adjoining the lands of Colin Poignant and Richart Henry; and this exchange was made for twelve shillings (soulz de tournois). This letter is sealed with the seal of the said viscounty in the year of our Lord 1316, the Saturday after the feast of Saint Gregory.

---

* Year 1334.— Sale of the above rent to the monks by Thomas Le Franc for a price of "trente sous de tournois."

Charter No. 11.

Abbey of Cerisy.

To all, as well present as future, know that I, *Alain Le François, of the parish of Tessy*, with the consent and will of Thomasse, my wife, have sold, conceded, and assigned to the ecclesiastical persons, my lords, the abbot and convent of Cerisy, one "sextier" of barley, measure of Tessy, to be taken every year from my fief, which I hold of them, in whichever place it may be, charging the said fief with the rent aforesaid, secure and without any prejudice to other revenue and boons, which the said ecclesiastical persons shall have as aforesaid from the said fief, which I, Alan aforesaid, and my heirs hold of them, and which is to be assigned every year for holding and enjoying it freely, quietly, and without being disturbed by the said ecclesiastical persons; and there will not be any trouble or disturbance on my part or my heirs or my wife in any manner whatever. And I am obliged to indemnify and guard from damage the said ecclesiastical persons, and in their interest have taken the oath of my wife. By this agreement the said ecclesiastical persons have paid 70 shillings (tournois argent), which is a good arrangement, because before I could not sell or alter the said heritage without their consent. In order that this charter may always remain irrefutable, I have appended my seal. Given in the year of our Lord 1272 the Sunday and feast of Saint James and Philip the Apostles before all the people of the parish of Tessy.

Chalmer refers to "Robert de Brus obtaining the grant of Annandale," and goes on to state, "As the charters of King David established a tenure by the sword, we may easily suppose that Bruce brought with him into the Annandale knights and yeomen from Yorkshire, as indeed might be shown by tracing to their origin some respectable families of Dumfrie-shire," so that it is not unreasonable to suppose that this *Robert Fraunceys* or one of his sons may have been an original settler with Bruce in the Annandale, and particularly so as you find a feudality existing, to which reference has already been made, according to the Scotch Records circa 1218, wherein it is stated "that *Roger, son of William Franciscus,* quit-claims to Sir Robert de Brus, Lord of Annandale, land which the grantee held of him in the territory of Annan, towards Weremundebi, for the excambion of land in the territory of Moffat, which *William Fran-ciscus,* the grantee's father, formerly held* of Sir Robert de Brus."

In this same epoch *Roger French (Francisco)* is a witness to a grant of Robert de Brus, Lord of Annandale, to William de Heneville. The grant is de-scribed as thirty-five acres of the grantor's demesne in the ville of Moffet, lying between the land of Sir

---

* This implies an earlier date of William F.'s possessions in Scotland.

Patrick, Earl of Dunbar, on one side, and the meadow of Sir Humphry de Kirkepatric on the other. This reference to the Earl of Dunbar recalls an agreement made on the 11th of November, 1218, "between" (the first) " P "(atrick), " Earl of Dunbar, and C "(hristina?), " the Countess, and Sir R "(obert) " de Brus " (probably son of William de Brus), wherein the consideration is that Sir Robert shall pay the money to the said earl and his said mother, C., the countess. In another charter, circa 1218, there is a resignation made to Robert de Brus where the name of *William Franceis* appears among the witnesses. At this period there is also a grant of the same Robert de Brus to Humphrey, son of Simon, where you find again among the witnesses *William Franceis.* The reference at this period to the possessions of Earl Patrick of Dunbar at Moffat in the Annandale and the relationship of his countess to Robert de Brus may account for the after feudal relations between the Dunbars and Frenches; and probably the first recorded mention of the name, appearing as a *witness to a charter* made by a member of the Dunbar family, was that of *William Franke de Pitcokyr,** of which the following is an abstract, found in the *cartulary of the Abbey of Coldstream*, edited by Rev. Charles Rogers.

---

* Pitcokyr gave at an earlier period the surname to a family which were vassals of the earls of Dunbar, but the reference to this place in this charter is the first instance the author has found wherein it is identified with the surname of Franke.

"*Mariota, Lady of Hume*, formerly spouse of Sir Patrick Edeger, in her lawful widowhood, has granted and quit-claimed all her right within the vill of Laynall and without it,—namely, of the 'Northtun,' with all its pertinents, to God and the Blessed Mary of Caldestrem, and the nuns there serving God,—as freely as any widow in the kingdom of Scotland in her viduity could grant or give, for a certain sum of money paid to her in her urgent necessity." Witnesses: "Domino Villelmo, vicario de Assinden, tunc magistro de Caldstrem; *Villelmo Franke de Petcokyr;* Malcolmo de Haukyrstun; Villelmo de Ardros, capellano; Thoma de Derchester; Alano Vyte de Derchester; et aliis."

Mariota, Lady of Hume, is recorded as the second wife of William de Hume, great-grandson of Cospatrick, third of this name, Earl of Dunbar. He was a son of William de Hume, who, after his lands, assumed his surname. Mariota afterwards, prior to the year 1284, married Sir Patrick Edgar. By the foregoing charter it appears that Mariota was then the widow of Sir Patrick Edgar; and, judging on the basis of the chronological rotation of this abbey's charters, it must have been made some time prior to the year 1289, the date of the death of Patrick, Earl of Dunbar, who is mentioned in the succeeding charter.

This is earlier than existing records of the *Frenches of Thornydykes;* and, from the fact that the Lairds

of that place had possessions in Petcoks in after
years, it is suggestive that *William Franke* may have
been an early member of the same family tree.

On the 28th of August, 1300–1, the records show
that *William Fraunceys* was a valet to Lord Patrick
(8th), *Earl of March;* and on the 18th of September
of the same year *Lord William le Fraunceys* was a
knight of the son of the *Earl of Dunbar.*

After the battle of Bannockburn, which took place
on the 24th of June, 1314, King Edward II. took
shelter in the first place of strength that was friendly,
which was the castle of Dunbar, where its lord was
still on the side of England; and it must have been
at this time that *William Fraunceys* rendered *at
Dunbar* the good service in King Edward's presence
for which he was rewarded by that monarch with
an annuity, as appears by a record on the 24th of
April, 1315.

Retracing our steps, it is found that the prototypes
of this surname in Scotland are discovered in the
reign of King William the Lyon; and probably the
first recorded early charter in Scotland in this king's
reign wherein the *surname of Franceis* is found as a
witness is that of *Grim to the Abbey of Melrose,* of
which the following is the translation: To all the
sons of the Holy Mother church as well present as
future. Grim son of Guido "caretarii de Roxburgh."
Greeting. Know that I for the welfare of my lord
Willielmus de Sumeruilla, and for my soul and for

the souls of my father, mother, and all my ancestors, have conceded and granted to God and the Holy Mother church of Melrose and the monks serving God there, the whole toft in Berwick, which I held of the said Willielmus as stated in his charter to me. And I have granted this land with all its appurtenances in the burgh and outside it, in free and perpetual alms, as freely, quietly, and fully as any other alms can be held, excepting only what is due lord Willielmus de Sumeruilla and his heirs by me and my heirs for the same land. And as I have no seal of my own for confirming and testifying to this my donation, Master Adam de Eccles has with my consent appended his seal to this my present charter. Witnesses: Magister Adam de Eccles; . . . capellanus; Ricardus de Dunst; Rogerus, filius Henrici; Randulphus de Cellario; Reinald de Hoyland; Willielmus clericus; . . . clericus; . . . Portman; Gocellinus Lunoc; *Willielmus Franceis;* Willielmus Albus; Johannes Niger; Willielmus Heem.

The next charter of interest in the " Liber Sancte Marie de Melros " is that of William de Hauccestestun, Richard, his brother, and others, conveying land in the territory of Innerwick (in Haddingtonshire) to the church of St. Mary of Melrose. Here, again, among the witnesses, apparently, is the name of the same, *William le Franceis.*

Three other charters without dates are found in the reign of this same king, in which the grantor was

Jocelin, Bishop of Glasgow. He was consecrated on the 1st of June, 1175, and died the 17th of March, 1199. These charters were in favor of the churches of Saint Mirini de Passelet and Saint Jacobus de Passelet, and all were witnessed by "*Wilelmus Francigena, capellanus Glasguensis.*"

Arnaldus Francigena is mentioned, circa 1200, in a charter of Arnaldus, the son of Peter de Kelso, to the church of St. Mary of Kelso. In describing the gift in the ville of Berwick, it is stated that the land is situated between that of *Arnaldus Francigena* and that of William de Bernahme.

In a charter of Herbert, son of Herbert of Chalmers, conveying land at Donipace to the church of St. Mary of Cambuskenneth,* in Clackmannanshire, about one-half a mile from Stirling, executed about the year 1200, *Adam Franceis* appears among the witnesses.

In another charter made in favor of the church of St. Mary of Melrose, circa 1200, by Hugh de Normanville and Alina, his wife, among the witnesses is the name of *William le Franceis.*

About the beginning of the reign of King Alexander II., and not later than 1227, *A. Francigena* was a witness to a charter of David Olyfard, to which his wife is a party, conveying the mill and certain land at Caders to the church and bishop of Glasgow.

---

* It was founded in 1145, and its canons came from Artois in France.

Circa 1232 *Willielmus Francus* (*Franco*) is one of the witnesses whose name is attached to a charter of John de Normanville, whereby he conveys to the church of St. Mary of Melrose and to the monastery in the same place all the lands, common of pasturage, and other easements which it claimed within the manor of Mackestoun under his father, Hugh de Normanville.

In another charter of about the same period the church and monastery of Melrose receive another grant from John de Normanville, *Willielmus Francus* appearing again among the witnesses.

Alan Franco is a witness to a grant by John de Crawfurd to the church of Newbottle of a portion of his land of Crawfurd, for the souls of his sovereign lord Alexander, King of Scots, and William, Malcolm, and David, his predecessors, etc. Not dated, but temp. Alexander II. (1214–49).

These charters are all in favor of abbeys and churches; and, with the exception of the churches of Glasgow and Passelet and the abbeys of Cambeskenneth and Newbottle, all are located in Tiviotdale, on the river Tweed, about ten miles to the southward of Thornydykes.

1291. Among the citizens of Berwick who took the oath of allegiance to King Edward I. on the 3d of June, 1291, was *Henricus Franceys*.

1294. *Andrew Franses* is a witness to a confirmation by James, the High Steward of Scotland, to the

Abbey of Paisley in Renfrewshire, of a quarry in that shire. The confirmation is dated at the Steward's manor of Blackhall in Renfrewshire. The witnesses are named in this order: Robert, Bishop of Glasgow; John Steward, the grantor's brother; *Andrew Frans'*; John de Soylus; Nicholas Campbell; Reginald de Crawfurd; Arthur de Donnon; knights, etc.

The name of *Sir William Fraunceys, knight*, is found several times about this period. One of this name swore fealty in the year 1296. There is also an agreement made in 1302 with Sir Rauf de Mantone, Sir Richard Siward, and the Council, in which Sir William Fraunceys arranged to keep the castle of Kirkintilloch until Christmas. Among his twenty-eight men at arms he had Sir Henry de Pinckeney, Thomas de Rameseye, and Gilbert de Menetethe. Besides, he had sixty foot soldiers, with a chaplain, petty officers, and artificers to repair the gate, drawbridge, and other defences, and the services of the tenants of the barony of Kirkintilloch on forays. He had his pay advanced until Christmas; and, whenever war should commence, he was to provide the castle with all necessaries. In 1304 he is mentioned as warden of this castle, and constable in 1305, and is again mentioned in 1306–7.

Roll of submission and fealty, in the year 1296, of John de Balliol, King of Scotland, with the clergy, nobles, and community of Scotland, to their liege lord, King Edward I. of England, renouncing the

league with the King of France. In this roll at
Forfarshire on July 4 appears the name of *Sir William Fraunceys, knight.* Afterward, on August 28, in
this same year and roll, in the Parliament of Nobles
and Prelates of both realms, held at Berwick-on-
Tweed, the same nobles, prelates, knights, and others
who had done homage *ut supra* at an earlier date,
with those hereafter named, again renounced the
league with France and did homage. Among these
of the surname were the following: —

> *John Fraunceys of Long Neuton, county of Roxburgh.*
> *John Fraunceys of Benestun, county of Edinburgh.*
> *William le Fraunceys, county of Edinburgh.*
> *Symon Fraunceys, county of Roxburgh.*
> *William Franceys, county of Fife.*
> *Aleyn Fraunceys, county of Roxburgh.*

An order for restoration seems to have been issued
by King Edward I., in the twenty-fourth year of his
reign, of the lands of John Bailiol, formerly King of
Scotland, and that of other lords and under-tenants.

On Sept. 3, 1296, a writ was issued to the sheriff
of Roxburgh to restore the lands of *Alan le Fraunceys and John le Fraunceys of Long Neuton.*

At this same date *Symon de Fraunceys,* tenant of
John Comyn of Badenagh, mentioned in the previous
roll, had his lands in county Roxburgh restored.

After the death of John Comyn there is still a
record of a *Symon Franceys,* whom we find in the

year 1306–7 among the four esquires of Sir Thomas de Multone, Lord of Egermund, in the barony of Couplaunde in Cumberland, who were for twelve days in the month of April of that year on an expedition to Glentrool * in search of Robert de Brus.

1311–12. *Richard Fraunceys and David Frauncis,* shield-bearers of Lord William de Kautone, knight, coming from Ireland on the mandate of the king, his lord, to the Scottish wars, with twenty-five men at arms, etc.

In 1312 King Edward II. of England, then at -York, appointed the following plenipotentiaries to treat of a peace with King Robert Bruce, which at that time was not accomplished, namely:—

William, Bishop of St. Andrews,

David, conte d'Asceles (Athole),

Patrick de Dunbar, conte de la Marche,

Alexander de Abernethy,

Adam de Gordon,

Gerard Salveyn,

and our dear clerks Meistre Robert de Pykeryng and *Meistre Johan Franceys,* canons of the church of St. Peter of York.

1312–13, March 14. Taking of Edinburgh Castle.

" The castle of Edinburgh had for governor Piers Leland, a knight of Gascony. Sir Thomas Randolph [nephew of King Robert Bruce] blockaded it

---

* A wild mountain lake in the upper part of Kirkcudbright.

so closely that all communication with the adjacent country was cut off. The garrison, suspecting the fidelity of Leland, thrust him into prison, and chose another commander in his stead. Matters were in this state, when *William Frank*, a soldier, presented himself to Randolph, his commander, and offered to show him how the walls of the castle might be scaled. The road, although amidst perilous precipices, had become familiar to him. Randolph, with thirty men, undertook the enterprise of scaling the castle at midnight. *Frank* was their guide, and the first who ascended the scaling ladder. Barbour states that 'Sir Andrew Gray followed him, and that Randulph himself was the third that mounted the ladder.' Before the whole party could reach the summit of the wall, an alarm was given, the garrison ran to arms, and a desperate combat ensued; but, their governor having been slain, the English yielded."

1313-14. Royal mandate, dated at Westminster, 18th of March, 1313-14, in regard the navy to be engaged in the war with Scotland.

William Fraunceys appointed chief of the royal vessel called "la Rodecogg."

1317. *Mariota Fraunceys* had her right of dower in all lands at Paxton, near Berwick-on-Tweed, forfeited by John de Cheseholme.

1306-29. *James Fraunces*, in the reign of King Robert I., held some feudatory rights over the lands of Burtries in the barony of Cunynghame and shire of Ayr, which had been granted by charter to Roger Blair.

King Robert Bruce (reign, 1306 to 1329) grants a charter to *William Franceis* of the 20 l. land of Sproustoun in Roxburghshire, which were in the king's hands by forfeiture of William Rict, Henry Drawer, Thomas Alkoats, John, Thomas, and William, sons of Alan, Hugo Limpetlaw. And the same king granted the barony of Sproustoun to his son, Robert Bruce. After the decease of this natural son the king granted the land of Sproustoun to *William Francis.* This latter charter was in the sixteenth year of his reign (1321–22).

1321. Thursday next before the feast of Saint Peter and Saint Paul. Inquest before the bailies of Berwick for the right of the Abbey of New-bottle to an annual rent of twenty shillings from tenements in Berwick. *Adam Frances* is on the inquest.

1329. *Master Francisco* had a donation from the king, and his expenses paid from Berwick to Dun-barton.

1335. *Adam Frensh* was among the Scotch patriots who were pardoned by King Edward III., at Berwick, on the 10th of October, 1335.

1335–36. Among the Scotch men at arms was *Johannes Frances.*

1335–36. In the account of this year of John de Stryvelyn, Viscount of Edinburgh, a yearly rent came from the land of *William le Frenshe, of Craumond,* in the viscounty of Edinburgh.

1336–37. Among the men at arms in the garrison of Edinburgh was *John Fraunceys.*

1337. Among the persons who contributed to the bridge at Berwick-on-the-Tweed were *Richard Fraunceys* and *John Fraunceys,* they giving both a certain yearly rental from tenements in the ville of Berwick.

Ayton.

This place lies about twenty miles to the eastward of Thornydykes and about nineteen miles from the castle of Dunbar, and was included in the shire of Coldingham, in which was located the priory of that name " whose records commence at an earlier period than those of any other monastery in Scotland." Among the many donators to this priory, the old Earls of March were particularly conspicuous, as it is to be observed by the many charters made by them in its favor; but David, the Baron of Quixwood, a territory adjacent to Coldinghamshire, seems to have outvied in his liberalities by charters most of the other donators. In the three charters herein recorded, it is noticed that *Adam Franceys* was a witness to all. As this search in the records of this priory is mainly confined to charters particularly

identified with the name of *Franceys*, whose possessions were at Ayton, this portion of the work will
have the title of

Franceys of Ayton.

Adam Franceys' name appears among the witnesses
to a charter of David, Baron of Quikiswde (Quixwood),
in favor of the church of Coldingham in Berwickshire,
wherein he grants land in the territory of Coldingham,
near to Stanlaulethe. As Bertram, prior of Coldingham, was also a witness, the date of this charter is
the latter part of the twelfth century, about the year
1188, at which time he was prior.

Adam Fraunceys appears again as a witness to the
following charters, to wit : —

Charter of Ricardus, son of Giliane de Lamberton,
to Stephanus, chaplain of Lamberton.

Charter of David de Quickesyd to the prior and
convent of Coldingham of land in the field of Coldingham, near Benerig.

Charter of Patricius, son of Helye Dunning, to St.
Mary of Coldingham of land in the ville of Renington, etc.

With the last three charters many of the witnesses
appear in the first charter herein named of David,
Baron of Quixwood, and in a record of 1235.

Charter of Symon, son of Thomas, of land at Eyton
to the office of almoner. The first witness to this
charter is Thomas, prior of Coldingham, which evi-

dently refers to Thomas Nisbet, who was prior from 1219 to 1239.

In the year 1235 we have a record of the services due the prior of Dunelmum (Durham) from Colding-hamshire; and among the individuals in this shire by whom such services should be rendered was *Adam le Fraunceys* and his heirs, for their land at Upper Ayton.

In the four succeeding charters, *Adam Fraunccys* is found again among the witnesses.

Charter of Willielmus de Lummesdene, with con-sent of Ermiger, his wife, of land in the territory of Coldingham to the monks in the same place.

Quitclaim given by Michael de Aldengrawe, son of Edward, to the prior and convent of Coldingham of land in the ville of Aldecambus.

Charter of David de Quickiswde of land in Dune-knol to the church of St. Mary of Coldingham. The first witness to this charter was Lord Anketino, the prior of Coldingham. This places the date of this charter during the time he held this office; and his occupation, according to M. Raine, was in 1239. The next prior seems to have been Richard, of which we have the date of 1245.

Charter of Richard, son of Elie de Prendergest, to Walter, his brother, of the husbandry of Leyroft.

With the preceding charters you find the orthog-raphy of these names, *Franceys, Fraunceys, Fraun-ceis, and Frances.*

Adam Franciscus and Thomas, his son, are both witnesses to a charter, in favor of Willielmus Frereman, of land in Coldingham, etc., granted by Mabilia, daughter of Constantinus.

In another charter of this same Mabilia, who is therein mentioned as a widow, land is given in Flores, in the territory of Coldingham, to the monks of Coldingham; and among the witnesses the names of the same individuals as are found in the preceding charter are given, as *Adam Fraunceys and Thomas, his son.*

This is the last record among these charters wherein the name of *Adam Fraunceys* appears; but in the year 1247 the name of *his son, Thomas Franceys,* only appears. This record, together with the fact that Richard, prior of Coldingham, was the first witness to this present charter, to whom M. Raine assigns the date of 1245, places the date of this charter at about that period.

Thomas Franceys.

Manumission in the year 1247 of Reginaldus, præpositus of Adam de Prendirgest, with the consent of Henricus, his son and heir. Among the witnesses to this document is *Thomas Franco.*

Charter of Willielmus, son of Beatrix de Swinton, wherein he granted to God, St. Ebbe, and the prior and monastery of Coldingham all the land, with appurtenances, which Walter (son of Leolphus), his grandfather, once held in the ville and territory of Swynton. Given in the full court at Ayton the day next after the feast of St. Martinus, anno gregoriense 1271. Witnesses: Dominus Henricus de Prendergest; Dominus Petrus de Morthintona, milites; Magister Hugo de Hertilpole; Willielmus Bel, tunc vicarius de Lamberton; Gilbertus de Lumisden; *Thomas Frances;* Alan de Swyntona; et alii.

Thomas and Richard Franceys of Ayton are witnesses to the charter of Alanus de Swinton (of Kirkecroft, in the territory of Swinton, wherein he mentions his wife Lucie) to the prior and monastery of Coldingham.

Charter of Henricus de Prendergest of land in Raynigton to the prior and convent of Coldingham, in exchange for the land which they gave him in the ville and territory of Prendergest. Dated at Ayton in the prior's court the seventh day of March, anno gregoriense 1275. Among the witnesses to this charter were *Richard Fraunc* of Ayton and *Thomas Fraunc* of Ayton.

Thomas Franceys of Ayton is a witness to a charter of Thomas, son of Robert, son of Mathew de Aldengrawe, granting land in the ville of Aldengrawe to the prior and monks of Coldingham. Given at the court of Ayton the day next before the feast of St. Dennis, in the month of March, 1275.

Charter of Willielmus, son of Willielmus Cantor

(chantor), in which he grants one toft with croft, etc., in Parva Ryston, to Alice, daughter of his sister Agnete and Augustinus. To this charter *Thomas Francys* of Ayton is among the witnesses.

Thomas Franceis of Ayton is among the witnesses to the charter of Nicholas Lambe, of land and tenement in Aldecambus: Know that I, Nicholas, son of Thomas of Aldecambus, have given and quitclaimed to God and the Holy Mary of St. Cuthbert, and to the prior and convent of Coldingham, all the land which I possess and will inherit in the ville and territory of Aldecambus, with escheat.

Quitclaim of the ville of Esteriston by Johannes, son of Bertramus of Esteriston, to the prior, etc., of Coldingham, in the year 1281. With the free will and consent of Robert, his son and heir, he quitclaims and restores the ville of Esteriston, with the lordship of same ville, etc., to the prior, etc. *Thomas Franč* of Ayton in this document appears as a witness.

In the rental of the possession of the monastery of Coldingham, which seems to have been empiled immediately after the year 1298, it is found that in Ayton Superior *Thomas Fraunceys* held two and one-half ploughlands, assessed for 100*s.* Forfeited, and in the prior's hands.

Richard Franceys.

This name appears among the witnesses to the charter of Nicholas, son of Thomas, son of Duncanus de Renington, in which he granted to Henricus de Prendergest, knight, all the land he possessed in the ville of Renington.

Pleading between Melrose and Coldingham. Anno gregoriense 1272, the day before Epiphany, was held a pleading between the monks, prior, and convent of Coldingham on one part, and the abbot and convent of Melrose on the other part, concerning the tithe to the fishery in Berwyc Stream, etc. Among the witnesses to this document is *Ricardo de Francisco of Ayton.*

Charter of Alice, formerly wife of Robertus, son of Mauricius, of Ayton Superior, in which she granted to Walterus, son of Robertus Purroc, and his heirs, all the land in the ville and territory of Ayton Superior which she had received as a dowry. Given at the full court of the prior of Ayton the day before the feast of Saint Mary, A.D. 1276. Here, again, you find *Ricardus Franc of Ayton* as a witness.

Ricardus Franceys of Ayton is among the witnesses to the charter of Emma, daughter of Elie Dunning, to Alanus carpentarius: —

Emma, daughter of the late Elye Dunnyng. Greeting. To all people, know that I have given, etc., to Alano carpentario and Mabille, his wife, my

niece etc., one toft and croft in the ville of Coldingham, near the wall of the monastery of Coldingham
to the south. Given at the court of Ayton the day of
March next after the feast of Saint Dennis, anno
gregoriense 1278.

Charter of Ade de Camera of land, with toft
in Ayton, to the prior and convent of Coldingham. Given at Ayton, the feast of Saint Gregory,
the Pope, in the month of March, anno gregoriense
1279. To this charter *Ricardus Fraunceys* is a
witness.

Charter of Robertus Hopp' (er) and Patricius, his
son, wherein they granted one acre of land in Coldingham, called Stampardesaker, to Stephanus de
Hoveden, then sexton of the church of Coldingham,
in free, etc., alms, for the sustenance of the chapel of
St. Ebbe, on the mountain. *Ricardus Fraunches* is
a witness. The first witness to this charter was
Lord Henry de Horncastle, then prior of Coldingham, which fixes the date of this charter not later
than 1276–96.

Charter of Thomas, son of the late Robertus Sene-
scallus of Coldingham, wherein he granted to the
monastery of Coldingham land in the moor toward
Lummesden, which formerly had been occupied by
Godricus, son of Willielmus Cocus, and all his land
in the same moor called Stiwardflattis. Among the
witnesses is *Ricardus Fraunceys.*

Charter of Lord Ricardus Frauncays of Ayton

Superior, wherein he granted his messuage with toft and croft in Ayton Superior for his maintenance (pro sustentacione sua) in the house of the monastery of Coldingham. Witnesses Dominis Henrico de Prendergest et Petro de eadem; Willielmo de Rokesburgh, tunc senescallo de Coldingham; Johanne filio Ade. Johanne Gray de Ayton; et aliis. This charter is most probably executed the latter part of the thirteenth century.

In the Rental of the Possessions of the Monastery of Coldingham, which seems to have been compiled immediately after the year 1298, it is found that in Ayton Superior *Ricardus Fraunceys* held six oxgangs of land, valued to 8*s.* yearly, which are in the hands of the prior.

Johannes Fraunceys.

Willielmus Ridel, Lord of Flemington, confirms the charter in which is granted one oxgang of land, with all that belongs to it, in the ville and territory of Flemington to Willielmus Stobbe, burgess of Berwick-upon-Tweede. Given at Flemington the fifth day of May, A.D. 1307. The name of *Johannes Fraunceys* appears among the witnesses.

Agreement of Johannes de Ayton with the monks of Coldingham. Given at Coldingham the day after the feast of Saint Laurence in the month of March, A.D. 1327. Among the six names given as witnesses attached to this charter was *Johannes Frankes.*

In 1350 *Adam le Fraunceys* * appears to have held land under William de Scaresburgh, prior of Coldingham. His widow Margaret at a later period gave four and a half acres of land in Flores to the arm's house of the priory.

On the 17th of August, 1403, King Henry IV. of England grants *Alexander Franche* some tolls of Berwick; and in 1407 *Alexander Franche* and his retainer Herteramus were both retainers of George, Earl of Dunbar, while in England. This same *Alexander Franche* is evidently referred to by King James I. in a charter of the 18th of February, 1426, as the grandfather of *James Franche.* In this charter the king grants to *James Franche* the land at Ayton, in the barony of Coldingham and county of Berwick which his grandfather Alexander had forfeited, probably at the same time as the forfeiture of George, Earl of March.

France of Linlithgow.

Johannes France, according to "Redditus Altarium Olim situat. infra Parochiam de Linlythgow," was a fuller by profession. He also held the office of *Burgess of the Burgh of Linlithgow* on the 22d of April,

---

* It is most probable this was the same person who is mentioned as Adam Francis on the inquest in the year 1321, in regard to tenements at Berwick, and again as Adam Frensh, who was pardoned in the year 1335 by King Edward III.

1487, as appears by the "Registrum Magni Sigilli Regum Scotorum." The situation of some of his tenements in this burgh are described in the "Redditus" to be found at the Advocates' Library, one of which is bounded on the north by the royal village, on the east by the land of William Hill, and that of Johannes Jak on the west. The inscription, formerly in the north aisle of the church of Linlithgow, evidently refers to this same individual:

> Heir lyes Ihon Franch, fadder to Tomas, Master
> Mason of Brig of Dee. Obiit anno Domini MCCCCLXXXIX.

Thomas Franche, the son, was the second *Master Mason to the Crown of Scotland.* He was appointed under the Privy Seal. The following is the grant conferring upon him the office of Master Mason, given by King James V. at Kelso on April 30, 1535:

"Ane letter given to *thomas franche* makand him maister masoun to oure souverane lord for all the dais of his lif wyth power to the said Thomas to vse and exercise the said office in all and by all thingis as ony vtheris vsit or exercit the samin in ony times bigane And therefor to haue yeirlie induring his liftyme of our said souerane lord the soume of £40 to be pait yeirlie be our souerane lordis treasurer now present and being for the tyme.— 30th April 1535.

Per signaturam."

Rev. Robert Scott Mylne, in his work on the "Master Masons to the Crown of Scotland," published in 1893, gives the pedigree of this family of Franch, with an account of Thomas Franche. The pedigree shows that the first of this surname was John Franche, who died in 1489; that Thomas Franche, his son, was Master Mason to the Bishop of Aberdeen for building the Bridge of Dee, and Master Mason to King James V. in 1535. This Thomas appears to have had three sons.

1st, Thomas, who died in 1530, and was buried in Aberdeen cathedral, where is found his epitaph. 2d, John, and, 3d, Robert, both masons, as appears by John Scrymgeour's account of 1538–39, under the heading of "Falkland" (the royal residence). This same account also mentions George Frensch.

Thomas Franche, senior, "after the death of his son Thomas, returned to his native town, and began to work for the King on the Palace of Linlithgow."

On the 22d of April, 1535, the King issued a warrant to the Master of Works to pay him a gratuity of £20 Scots for the satisfaction given in his work for the past year, to wit: "At Linlithgow, 22d April 1535.— Master of our wark, for samekyll as Thomas Franche maison hes beyne continuallye in our service for the completing our Palis of Linlithquhow sen Merche wes ane yeir and hes done us for his part greit pleasour thairintyll quhilk we think deservis revard. Heirfor it is our will and als chargis you incontinent to deliver to the said Thomas £20 for his bontay and the samyn salbe weil allowit to you in your comptis. Subscrivit be us at Linlithquhow, the xxij day of Aprile, and of our regne the xxij yeir. JAMES R."

On the 30th of April of this same year, as previously stated, he received the appointment of Master Mason.

"Accounts of the Master of Works, 16 May 1535. One pound Scots to the Master Mason, weekly, and Masons 16ˢ. and 12ˢ. weekly."

"The compt of the masonis that wrocht at the palis of Linlithgow as eftir followis: — The first day of Februar the yeir of God jᵐvᶜxxxiiij yeris the entres of Thomas Franss * masoun with ten masonis and four barrowmen with him. And tha continewit to the xvj day of Maij in the year of God jᵐvᶜxxxv yeris, the quhilk is 15 vokkis. To the said Thomas Frans * voklie 20ˢ, and, to four of his masonis ilkane of thame 15ˢ vokle and to sax of his masonis ilkane of thame 12ˢ voklie, and to ilkane of his barrowmen vokle, 5ˢ Summa to the said Thomas Frans * and his servandis vokle £8: 16ˢ. Summa of thir personis forsaidis vagis in the haill £132."

"Item, to the said Thomas Frans * at the command of our Soverane lordis precept £20."

---

* This orthography is given in Mylne's "Master Masons," but Frans (or Franss) is evidently a contraction for Franses. Records show that Robert France of the Stane had his surname written Franses and Francys.

" In 1537 work was recommenced on the Palace of Falkland," and "at first Thomas Franche plays an important part in the royal undertaking." In March, 1537–38, works were undertaken on the Garden Dyke, by the King's command.

In the year 1538–39 you find a record of two of his sons, in which the orthography of this surname is Frensch.

Thomas Franche was living on the 31st of July, 1551, and appears to have died the same year.

There appears to have been a *John Franche* identified with *Falkland,* the Royal Residence, most probably a relation. Under the date of the 7th of November, 1592, is the following entry : —

"*Gift to John Franche* for his true and thankful service done to the King, of the office of building and upholding the park dykes and meadow dykes of Falkland, for life."

George Frensch, to whom reference is made in this present article, may have been the same person who held land in or near Aberdeen on the 10th of February, 1474–75.

Before closing these general remarks, reference will be made to the following records of the border counties of England, which historically are much interwoven with Scottish history.

In December, 1231, *John Francigena* gives the K.

20 marks, to have for life the close of the border (costera) of Warnel, which the abbot of Holcoltram enclosed and held in hand, and the ten acres of said wood which the abbot assarted and cultivated by the K.'s license, for half a mark to be paid to the K. annually, as the abbot paid for the same, as fully contained in his charter; and Thomas de Muleton is commanded, after taking security, to give him seizin.

On Dec. 26, 1231, the K. grants to the church of the Blessed Kentigern of Caldebec, and *John Francigena, parson thereof,* and his successors, the close of the "costera" of Warnel, which the abbot of Holmcoltram, by the K.'s license, enclosed and held during pleasure, paying half a mark to Exchequer annually.

Cumberland.— Walter, Bishop of Carlisle (Thomas fitz John for him), renders his account: *John Francigena* accounts for 20 marks to have in perpetuity a close of the "costera" of Warnelle, which the abbot of Holcoltram enclosed and held in hand, and to have ten acres of same wood which the said abbot cleared and cultivated by the K.'s license, for half a mark to be paid to the K. annually, as the said abbot paid for these acres and close, as more fully contained in the K.'s charters, and in his own charter thereof, a transcript of which is attached to the "Originale" of the 17th year, bearing that the said close and ten acres of land shall forever remain with the said John and his successors, parsons of the church of the Blessed Kentegern of Kaldebec. He has paid it into the treasury, and is quit. (Pipe, 16 Hen. III. [1231-32], Rot. 15, dorso.)

On the 10th of February, 1232-33, Thomas de Muleton of Egremund is commanded to take in the K.'s hand the ten acres of the border of the K.'s wood of Warnel, and the close, which the abbot of Holcoltram held and the K. afterwards gave to *John le Franceis, parson of Caldebec,* by charter, and hold them till further orders. Westminster.

Pleas at Westminster in the octaves of Saint Michael, before Robert de Lexington and other justices. Westmoreland: *John le Franceys* appears versus Johanna de Veteripont in a plea that she should restore him the custody of William de Pinkeny's land and heir, whereof she unjustly deforced him. She is absent. Judgment,—let her be attached for the octave of Saint Hilary. (Coram Rege, 26 and 27 Hen. III. No. 55, m. 6.)

Pleas at Westminster (in a month from Holy Trinity). Westmoreland: *John le Frannceys* appears by attorney versus Robert de Veteripont in a plea that the latter should acquit him of service which John de Bayllot exacts from him for the freehold he holds of Robert in Maldesmebrunne, whereof Robert as the "medius" between them should acquit him. Robert is absent. Attached to attend on the morrow of Saint Martin. (Coram Rege, 34 Hen. III. No. 82, m. 14, dorso.)

On the 30th of September, 1251, in the pleas of

the assizes of the county of York, it is found that Robert, son of Ivo de Veteripont, acknowledged that he had granted to John de Baylof * (Balliol) and his heirs the homage and service of *John le Fraunceys* † for Florliswrth in the county of Leicester, and likewise the homage and service of *said John* for the moiety of the *manor of Soureby* ‡ in Farnes in *Galloway* (Galewaythe), as more fully contained in the writing made between them.

On the 2d of April, 1255, in the division made of the possessions in Northumberland by the king's escheator of the lands of Isabella de Forde, which she had inherited from her grandfather Robert de Muscamp, through his eldest daughter, Cecilia, it is found that her heirs were her aunt Isabella, the wife of William de Huntercumbe, and her two cousins, Muriel and Margery, daughters of her aunt Margery, who had married Malise, Earl of Stratherne. These possessions were divided in two portions, the records

---

* He married Dervorgilla, youngest daughter of Alan, Lord of Galloway. She was the mother of King John Baliol and Margory, who married John Comyn of Badenach.

† John Le Fraunceis was the son of Hugh Le Fraunceis. He held land in some of the northern English counties, one manor at least under Robert de Veteripont. His name appears again in the records of the county of Cumberland in the years 1253 and 1258.

‡ The church of Great Soureby was granted to Dryburgh Abbey at the end of the twelfth century by Ivo de Veteripont, in pure alms, and was confirmed to it by Roland, Lord of Galloway, under whom Ivo de Veteripont held the land of Great Soureby.

of the first showing that *Robert le Franceys* held of
the said Isabella de Forde possessions in the burgh
of Wllouer (Wooler) in Northumberland.

Among the Cumberland records under the date of
the 26th of May, 1256, it is found that *Nicholas le
Fraunceys* was among the men of Alan de Moleton
(Muleton) and Alicia, his wife, daughter of Richard
de Lucy and Ada Moreville, who afterward married
Thomas de Multon, of Egermund.

On the 18th of August, 1268, *Gilbert le Fraunceys*
is among the *belted knights* who were, with others,
on the inquest held at the castle of Maidens in
the king's forest of Engilwode, before Roger de
Lancastre, then seneschal of the king's forests ultra
Trent, and William de Dacre, then sheriff of Cumberland, and others of the king's lieges, in regard to
certain rights of King Henry III. in Cumberland.

A *Gilbert le Fraunceys* is mentioned in the records
of Cumberland, in the year 1259, as the *son of Richard
le Franceys*. From the year 1273 to 1278 there are
records of *Gilbertus le Franceys* holding large possessions in Chester, Cumberland, Derby, Leicester, and
Westmoreland.

As this account is so general on these surnames
in Scotland, with a special and long account of the
Frenches of Thornydykes, it seems only appropriate
that some additional allusion be made to two other
families,— those of *Francys of Stane* and the *Frenches
of Frenchland.* The last of the line of Stane was

Elizabeth, only daughter and sole heiress of Robert Francys, or France, of Stane, or Stonanrig, in the parish of Irvine, in Ayrshire, who married, in 1508, William Montgomery of Greenfield. An interesting account of this family is found in the " History of the County of Ayr," by James Paterson.

In regard to the Frenches of Frenchland, in the Annandale, those interested can easily refer to that admirable work called "*Alexander Nisbet's Heraldic Plates,*" *so successfully completed by Messrs. Ross and Grant, members of the Lyon Office.*

As a prelude to the introduction of the Frenches of Thornydykes in Berwickshire, one of the border counties of Scotland, it seems an appropriate occasion to revive in our memories what *Sir Walter Scott* says about this historic and picturesque region. His name has a special interest to those of the surname of French, from the fact that he had, as *one of his tutors, James French.*

The border of Scotland, in which was the home of the Frenches, is described most interestingly by Sir Walter Scott: " The Scotch Border has charms to fascinate all those who delight in romantic enterprise and poetic fancy. This boundary between two warlike and long hostile kingdoms became naturally the great theatre on which the achievement of the feudal ages were performed. The habitual hostility, too, with which the inhabitants of the opposite side of the March view each other, gave rise to constant scenes of minor exploits, which, though they could not find a place in history, kept alive the habits of activity, enterprise, and daring valour, which held men's minds in a state of perpetual excitement. The same causes which rendered the Borders the theatre of war rendered it also a land of song; for true and native poetry is the result, not of monastic and studious seclusion, but of those eventful circumstances which fire the imagination, and melt the heart."

A descriptive account of the Merse is given by Mr. Browne in his "Glimpses in Lammermuir": "Before leaving the shelter of the old firs of Hardens Hill, Willie gazed down into the Merse. There it lay before him, with its long and broad sweep of farm-land, dotted with villages, farm steadings, mansions, and wood, and bounded on the far south by the grey Cheviots, at whose feet, thirteen and fifteen miles away, if his ear could have carried sound as his eye did sight, he might have heard the Tweed roaring through the bridges of Coldstream and Norham, and then rushing between its banks at Ladykirk, and onwards to the sea, where the waves on the Berwick beach rolled up as if in joy to meet it. If the dusk had come suddenly down, Willie, in his statuesque position, might have started at the appearance of a flaring light far away on the Farne Isles, to caution the watch at the forecastle of the labouring ship miles away at sea, as he gazed forward into the dark and heaving billows. But now, as he reached the highest

point of the road, and as he left the lowland land-
scape behind him, another and not less striking
scene, but of a diverse character, burst upon his view.
Spread out before him, as if by the hand of an en-
chanter, was a wild and extensive piece of Highland
scenery, and, as he rounded the road and pressed
forward, its extent increased. The Lammermuirs,
in rolling billows of heather hill and pasture land,
stretched for many miles on three sides, and conspicuous in the distance on the left was the ancient
castle of Hume, and the three peaks of the Eildon
Hills due south-west, seventeen miles away."

PART SECOND.

FRENCHES OF THORNYDYKES.

FIRST LAIRD OF THORNYDYKES.

Robert French, the first Laird of Thornydykes *
on record, received, according to Nisbet, a principal
charter from George Dunbar,† Earl of March, Lord
of Annandale, "upon his resignation in the Earles
hands for a new infeftment to himself and his wife
Elizabeth in conjunct fie and the heirs of their bodie,
which failyeing to Adame French sone to Robert,
and his heirs male, which failyeing to airs whatsome-
ever." "In which charter the Earle designes the said
Robert French of Thorndyke *Clarissimŭs consan-
guineus noster.*"

---

* Thornidicke, Thorne Dykes, Thornydyke, or Thorndie Castle
or Tower in the district of Thornydykes was a place of defence.
A later description gives it besides a manor house, gardens,
orchards, dovecots, with estates in tenancy and service of free-
holders, mills, mill lands, mill fees, etc. Its location was in the
Merse, near the foot of the Lammermoor Hills, in what is now
called the parish of Westruther; of old, it was near the religious
houses of Wedderlie and Bassendean, in the extended parish of
Home; at the Reformation, which began in 1560, it became part
of the parish of Gordon. The site of this tower was to the south
of Spottiswood, on the northern side of the road leading from
Greenlaw to Lauder.

† The earldom of March was confirmed to him by King David
II. on the resignation of Patrick, ninth earl, July 25, 1368.

SECOND LAIRD OF THORNYDYKES.

Adam French, second Laird of Thornydykes, succeeded his father Robert in the reign of Robert III. (19th April, 1390–4th April, 1406); and Nisbet makes the following allusion to the succession: "This appears by ane other charter upon resignatione of his mother Elizabeth French [who is surnamed French in this but not in the former] in favour of his [Robert's] son and his spouse, Jonet Rule, of the same contents with the former [charter] in the hands of the foresaid George, Earl of March, and Lord of Annandale and Man."

About this period Adam Gordon,* William Baird, and Adam French became conspicuous among the border chieftains; for at a meeting held in 1398 between the Commissioners of the Scotch and English marches, appointed to arrange about border difficulties, prisoners, etc., an exception was made to the release of these persons. At that the Scotch Commissioners gave heavy bonds in the name of their

---

* The history of the Gordon family at this period shows only one of this Christian name, that of Sir Adam Gordon, Lord of Gordon and Huntly, who was killed at the battle of Homildone Hill in Berwickshire, Sept. 14, 1402.

king for their appearance before the ensuing meeting of the Lord Commissioners of both realms, and
agreed they should not violate the truce in the in-
terval. Evidently owing to the complications grow-
ing out of the frontier difficulties, in which the border
lords of both countries were generally equally respon-
sible, the ill feelings engendered by their constant
attacks on each other, often without even the provo-
cation of open warfare, and with the apparent in-
ability or indifference of the two kings to suppress at
times these local troubles, which often involved the
peace of both kingdoms, with these lawless but not
unusual state of affairs for these early days, and with
the apparent desire on the part of King Robert III. to
preserve peaceful relations with his formidable neigh-
bor, King Richard II., Adam French is presumed to
have been among those selected as an example; for he
suffered the penalty of the forfeiture of his estates of
Thornydykes and Pitcoks. George, Earl of March,
the direct feudal lord of Adam French, renounced his
allegiance to King Robert III. in 1399; and it must
have been about this period, after the forfeiture of his
estates, that Adam French abandoned the Scottish
king. Earl George, Gaweyn, his son, and Adam
French about the same period became liegemen of
King Henry IV. of England; and all received annu-
ities from him. It is not at all unlikely that Adam
French went to England in 1400 in the company of
his overlord, the Earl of March; for on August 2 of

that year George of Dunbar, Earl of March, received from the English king safe conduct and protection for himself, his wife, and his children, with a retinue of eighty persons coming to England. The exact date of his becoming liegeman is not known; but on April 7, 1402, there is a record of Adam French of Scotland, showing that he was then in the service of the King of England, and that he had been granted an annuity, and on the 17th of July, 1403, he received from King Henry IV. a prest of his annuity for his good service. There seems to be nothing to show the exact date when Adam French returned to Scotland; but he evidently seceded from England, and came back to his Scottish allegiance. After the forfeiture of Adam French, Robert French, his son, had a charter from King Robert III. of Thornydykes and Pitcoks; but Adam French, the father, became repossessed of these estates, as appears by a charter of confirmation of King James I., dated at Edinburgh on the sixth day of January, 1433, and he must have soon after died, as his son Robert succeeds him, as appears by the inquest held in the latter part of January of that year.

Notes on individuals of this surname, etc.

Andrew French. In the time of Robert III. (1390-1406) is a charter to Andrew French of the lands of Boudington, within the barony of Cunynghame and shire of Ayr.

Gilbert Franche was a witness at Edinburgh on the 7th April, 1401, to an instrument of assignation by Thomas de Altoun of a tenement at Musselburgh to Henry Bollow, burgess there.

Gilbert Franche is also among the witnesses to a public document dated at Edinburgh on the 8th of January, 1437.

Robert French, third Laird of Thornydykes, was
son of Adam French. He succeeded to the forfeited
estates of his father, as it appears by a charter to him
from King Robert III.,* of the lands of Thornydykes
in the shire of Berwick, and Petcokkis † in the shire
of Edinburgh. As Lord of Thornydykes, he appears
as a witness to the confirmation of a charter to the
church of Cavers, dated at the church of Makerston
(both located in the county of Roxburgh), on July 29,
1406. Allusion has been made to Adam French, his
father, temporarily gaining possession of these estates
in 1433; but Robert French came again in possession of the estates of Thornydykes and Pitcoks, as
appears by the following record of the inquest: —

"Robert succeeds his father Adam, and is served

---

* In his reign owners of land were required to show their charters for land held.

† Pitcokkes, Petcokyr, Petcoke, Pitcoks, or Pitcox, was located
near Dunbar Castle, in the barony of Bele and earldom of March,
and about seventeen miles from Thornydykes (now in Stenton
Parish). This estate, in the reign of King James VI., comprised
manor house, dovecots, workshops, breweries, mill land, mill fees,
game and fish preserves, peat bogs, coal, ponds, stream, woods,
meadows grazing, and pasture lands, stone quarries, and lime pits.

and retoured to him the 29 of Januarie, 1433,* at Dunbar."

His eldest son was Robert, who succeeded him; but the Frenches of Frenchland record for him a younger son, James, who is represented as their ancestor.

---

* Johannes de Fraunce.

About this period — namely, in the years 1429 and 1431 — safe conduct and protection was granted by Henry VI. to Johannes de Fraunce; and in the second record he is mentioned as John Fraunce. In both these documents, he is named as retainer of Andrew Keith of Inverugie, on his way to England to see his lord, who was one of the hostages for King James I. of Scotland.

A Johannes Fraunce is found in an account of John Maxwell, Steward of Annandale, given at Perth the tenth day of July, 1459, of all the income and expenses of his bailiwick from the twenty-seventh day of June, 1458, to the day of this account. It is found that Johannes Fraunce was fined for being absent from court.

Robert French, the fourth Laird of Thornydykes.
On the 22d of October, 1478, "the Lordis decretis
that Johne Hume of Cralin, Robert Fransche of
Thornydikis, Johne of Quhitsum, Alexander Hume,
Patric Michel, James Fransche, and Jok Lawsoun,
sall restore and deliver againe to Dene William
Rothŭen, chanoun of Driburgh, for twa horssis and
twa sadillis, that thai spulzeit fra the said chanoun
VIJ.^{lib} and that thai sall for the contempcioune done
to the Kingis Hienes in the takin of the said horssis
and strikin of the said chanon, entir thair personis in
warde in the Castell of Blacknes and remayne thair

Notes on individuals of this surname, etc.
Lord Johannes Franche. In several charters of William
Striveling of Keir, in the viscounty of Perth, having the confirmation of King James III., Johannes Franche, chaplain, is among
the witnesses. In the first two charters, dated at the manor
of Ker on the 28th of July, 1477, he is called Lord Johannes
Franche. In the charter of the 27th of September, 1477, dated at
the same manor, he is called Johannes Franche, chaplain. In
the two charters dated at Edinburgh on the 25th of June, 1479,
he is called Johannes Franche, chaplain.
Lord Nicholas Franche. Confirmation charter by King James
IV. to a charter of the late Thomas de Carmichell, vicar of the
parochial church of Stirling, in favor of Lord Nicholas Franche,

on thair avin expenssis quhill thai be fred be the king."

---

chaplain, and his successors, the chaplains, who shall serve God at the altar of St. Michael the Archangel, in the parochial church of S. Cross, in the burgh of Stirling. Dated at latter place 1st of April, 1471.

On the 15th of November, 1475, marriage was solemnized in face of the kirk between Duncan Aquhonam and Agnes Makcalpyn, by Sir Nicholas Franch, curate of the parish church of Strivelin, within the parish church of the Holy Road of the burgh, the parties giving oath as above: whereupon an honorable man, William Stewart' of Baldoran, and Malcolm M'Clery of Garten, gave their corporal oaths that the said Duncan was of lawful age to contract marriage with the foresaid Agnes M'Calpin. Done in the said church the fifth hour before noon or thereby.

In the Records of the Royal Burgh of Stirling, under dates of the 3d of March, 1476–77, and the 5th of May, 1477, may be found the name of Sir Nicholas Franche, curate of Stirling.

William Franche. 1480, June 23. The Lords decern that William Franche shall pay to Franskin Fersandris, procurator for Merlin Puis, viij^{lib}, due by his obligation, and ordain that letters be written to distrain him for the said sum.

1480, June 30. The lords of council decern that William Franche shall pay to copin Van Re, procurator for Peter Densmond, the sum of iij^{lib}, due by the said William Franche.

Sir Jhone Franche. 1484, July 27. In the actioun by Sir Jhone Franche, chaplain, against Robert Noble of the Ferme, for the spoliation of half of the lands of Ballioffra, etc., the lords decern against the said Robert Noble, etc.

There appears to have been a Sir John Franche who is mentioned on the 22d of June, 1492, in the action pursued by Malcolm Drummond and Mergaret Muschet, spouse of John the Graeme, against James Muschet of Tolgart, etc. It was alleged for the said James Muschet that the assignation under the sign of Sir John Franche was given with an antedate after the said Mergaret had discharged him of the sum of xxjj^{xx} merkes.

FIFTH LAIRD OF THORNYDYKES.

Robert French, fifth Laird of Thornydykes. On the 8th of March, 1490, in the action and cause pursued on behalf of our soverign lord and Archibald Boid in Smalem, against Thomas Rutherford, Robert Franche of Thornydike, and others, the lords of council decern and ordain, if it please the said Archibald, that the inquest be changed to a new day.

Notes on individuals of this surname, etc.

George Franche. In a charter of Henry Munduail (Mundwell) confirmed by the king, dated at Bigare, Lanark, on the 30th of September, 1486, the name of George Franche appears among the witnesses. This charter conveys land in the ville of Mertoun, in the viscounty of Berwick, to Johannes Hume of Quhutrig.

A George Franch is recorded in 1508–9, 5 February. Action at the instance of Margaret Gordon, daughter to Alexander, Earl of Huntlie, against Rolland Leirmontht, Robert Brone, Alexander Wod, Patrick Wod, Alexander Wod, younger, Thomas Alexander son, Patrick Home, George Franch, and Thomas Huntle, for the wrongous occupation of her lands lying within the lordship of Gordon. Continued till 4 March next.

SIXTH LAIRD OF THORNYDYKES.

Adam French, sixth Laird of Thornydykes, had saisine of Thornydykes and Pitcox in 1494.

Another record appears of him on the 16th of December, 1503, in the action and cause pursued on behalf of the king against Adam Franch of Thornydikes, and others serving upon a breive of inquest impetrate by Walter Haliburnton by the decease of William Haliburnton of Mertoun, upon £20 worth of land lying in the town of Merton and sheriffdom of Berwick, for their wilful error and unjust deliverance that the said lands were held in blenchferme. Their decreet is therefor held as of no avail, force, or effect in time to come.

A record appears again on the 19th of December, 1505, in an action and cause pursued at the instance of the king, and of George, Master of Angus, against James Aldincraw, Sheriff Depute of Berwick, Adam Franch of Thornidikis, James Spottiswod of that Ilk, and the remainder of the persons that were upon the serving of a brief of inquest impetrate by George Roule by the decease of George Roule, his father, of the lands called Edmondis field, lying within the sheriffdom of Berwick.

There is a certain amount of suspicion that
this Adam French may have retired, and entered
the church; for in the year 1526, as hereafter

Notes on individuals of this surname, etc.

Thomas Franche, marshal. In the Exchequer Rolls of Scotland, David Hoppringle of Smailhame, ranger of (the warden)
the Tweed, renders his account from the 6th of July, 1497, to the
4th of July, 1498, wherein a payment of 20 pounds is made to
Thomas Frainche, one of the marshals of the royal household.
In the account rendered in 1499 by Sir Duncan Forrester, knight,
Thomas Franche, marshal, again received compensation. The
account rendered at Stirling on the 12th of March, 1499–1500, by
Sir Patrick Hume of Polwarth, knight, shows another payment
made to Thomas Franche, marshal. John Striveling of Crag-
bernarde shows, in his account of 1503, an entry of a payment
made to Thomas Franche, marshal. A similar payment was made
in 1508; and in the statement of Alexander, Lord of Hume,
chamberlain of the land of the barony of Haliburton, given at
Edinburgh on the 11th of July, 1509, 10 marks in feod are given
to Thomas Frainche, marshal. There is still another account
which was rendered in the same year by Sir Duncan Forrester
of Garden, wherein it is recorded that 20 marks were allowed to
Thomas Franche, marshal.

William Frank. In 1502 Willielmus Frank has saisine of
Frankysland in Pebles.

Thomas Franche. Thomas Franche had a gift from King
James IV. on the 23d of December, 1506, of the movable goods,
etc., of the deceased John Setoun, alias Cuke.

Thomas Frank, chaplain. Among the records relating to the
High School of Edinburgh, which was located in the Vennel of
the church of St. Mary in the Fields, under the date of August,
1508, Magister Thomas Frank is among the witnesses, and again
a witness on the 23d of October, 1512. By another document, dated the 24th of January, 1516, it is found that Johannes
Irland, bailiff, transferred a certain yearly rental to a discreet
man, Master Thomas Frank, chaplain, one of the prebendaries of
the said Collegiate Church of St. Mary in the Fields, for a mass

stated, he was succeeded in the estates of Thornydykes by Robert, the seventh Laird; and in this
same year you find Sir Adam Frenche * preb-

---

to be celebrated yearly on a certain day at the altar, founded by
Master David Vocat, for his soul and those of his parents. On
the 25th of September, 1526, Master Thomas Frank, chaplain,
is among the witnesses to a record relating to the aforesaid
High School of Edinburgh.

Megote Franche. The name of Megote Franche appears in
a charter of the 20th of May, 1511, dated at Dumblane, in Perth-
shire, wherein it is stated she held some property in that city.

Sir William Franche. 12th of June, 1521. Election of Sir
David Yhong to the first prebend in the church of St. Giles at
Edinburgh, vacant by the death of Sir William Franche.

* Sir Adam Frenche. 12th of April, 1526. Sir Adam Frenche
is a witness to an act of the chapter of the Holy Trinity Collegiate Church.

1531, May 1. Sir Adam Franche is a witness to charter by
John Dingwall, provost of the Kirk of the S. Trinity, near Edinburgh, and clerk of the parish of Soltie.

King James V. confirmed a charter of Jonete Kennedy, Lady
of Bothuile, wherein she, with the consent of M. Richard Bothuile,
provost of the Collegiate Church of Blessed Virgin Mary in the
Fields, with its prebendaries and chapter, and King James and
Jacobus, archbishop of St. Andree, for the soul of her late husband, etc., founded a prebend in the Collegiate Church under the
walls of Edinburgh, and granted for its maintenance the land
formerly a tenement of the late Hugo Bar, together with the land
and houses to the south of the royal village in le Nudryswynd,
etc. To this charter, dated at Striveling the 16th of May, 1531,
Adam Frenche, prebendary of the Collegiate Church of the Holy
Trinity, was among the witnesses.

Sir Adam Frenche, chaplain, 12th of February, 1543-44.

1544, Nov. 29. Adam Frenche signs grant with the other
clergy of the Collegiate Church of Trinity.

Charter by Adam Frensche, sacristan and prebendary of the
Collegiate Kirk of the Holy Trinity near Edinburgh, in favor of

endary of the Collegiate Church of the Holy
Trinity.

Children of the Sixth Laird.

First, Robert French, who succeeds.

Second, John French, who is referred to in the
Regist. Secreti Sigilli as follows: "Ane lettre maid
to Johnne Franche, bruthir to vmquhile Robert
Franche of Thornydykis, his airis and assignais,
ane or ma of the gift of the Releif of the landis of
Thornydykis, and Petcokis with partis and pendiclis
thairof, and all thair pertinentis, and of all vthir
landis quhilkis pertenit to the said vmquhile Robert
aucht and pertening to our souerane Lady for sesing
gevin or to be gevin to Adam Franche, sone and air
of the said vmquhile Robert of the samyn. And
als of the gift of the mariage of the said Adam, sone
and air foirsaid, and failzeing of him be deceis vn-
marut the mariage of ony vthir air or airis, male or
female, of the said vmquhile Robert that sal happin
to succeid to him in his landis and heretage with all
proffittis of the said mariage, with power, etc. At

Isabelle Cokburn, relict of John Wardlaw of Ricarton, and now
spouse to David Kincaid of Coates, of the lands of Hill in the
barony of Balerno and shire of Edinburgh. At the said college
the 21st of February, 1545–46.

Sir Adam Franche appears as a witness to an act of the
chapter of the Holy Trinity Collegiate Church on the 17th
of March, 1548–49.

Edinburgh the XXV. day of Januar, the yeir of God one thousand five hundred and forty-eight.

Per signaturam."

John Franche was party to a marriage contract in the year 1549.

Third, Alexander Frenche. At Edinburgh, on the 20th of February, 1539, the name of Alexander Frenche appears among the witnesses to a charter of Jacobus Striveling de Keir, which was confirmed by the queen on the 18th of April, 1550.

Alexander Franche (and George Franche) are among the witnesses to a charter of Jacobus Striveling, son and heir of the late Johannes Striveling de Kere, knight, in favor of David Huntar of Newtoun, and Magaret Wod, his wife, of land of Balcarres with tenancy and mill, etc., in the lordship and viscounty of Fiffe, dated at Edinburgh on the 8th of June, 1540, which the king confirmed at Falkland on the 14th of August, 1541.

Again the name is found as a party to a marriage contract on May 18, 1549, which was recorded on the 23d of June following.

Fourth, George Franche. His name appears as a witness to the charter of the 8th of June, 1540. He was on the side of the Kers in the feud existing between them and the Scotts, and was designed of Thornydykes on Dec. 3, 1549, in a summons at the instance of Walter Scott of Branxholme.

This name occurs among the witnesses on the 3d of November, 1551, to a charter of William Lindesay, son and heir of the late Robert Lindesay, burgess of Edinburgh, in favor of Johannes Hammiltoun and his heirs and assigns, of the land of Strikfeild, in the vis-county of Peblis, this charter having the confirmation of Queen Mary on the 18th of November following.

NOTE. Katrina Franche was one of the nuns who signed the election of Jonet Hoppringill as prioress of Coldstream on Feb. 23, 1537-38.

Robert French, seventh Laird of Thornydykes,
succeeded his father, Adam. "Came in possession
of the estates, according to Chancery Books, in
1526"; found among the barons and lairds of Berwickshire in 1530; on May 20, 1538, he is on an
assize in apprising of lands in Graden, in Berwickshire; mentioned again on the 10th of April, 1546;
and appears to have died before the 25th of January,
1548.

Robert French married Anne Hume, a member of
the patriotic, poetical, and religious family living at
Polwarth, near by in the same shire. Her aunt, Margaret Hume, was lady abbess of North Berwick.
Her brother, Patrick, the fifth baron of Polwarth,
"left specimens of poetry which seem to have been
popular in the court of James VI., to which he
was attached. He was a great promoter of Reformation, and on the breaking out of the Civil War
he sided with the young king." Adam Hume, a
younger brother, distinguished by his virtue and
probity, was the first Protestant rector of the church
of Polwarth, while Swinton in his privately printed

work on the " Men of the Merse " states that another
" brother, Alexander, was the author of a volume of
hymns and sacred songs breathing a spirit of piety
worthy of his calling as a minister of the gospel,
which he exercised for eleven years at Logie, near
Stirling," on the river Forth. Margaret Home, her
sister, married John Baillie of St. John's Kirk, in
county Lanark.

Her father was Patrick, fourth baron of Polwarth,
and her mother, Elizabeth, daughter of Sir Patrick
Hepburn of Wauchtoun, in county Haddington.

Hue French, the son of Robert French, in his will
of 1574 mentions a half brother and sister, David and
Jonet Swinton. There are no indications that Anne
Home was a widow Swinton before she married
Robert French, or that he married a widow of this
surname; but it is most probable that on the demise
of Robert French, whose death took place prior to
25th of January, 1548, that his wife, Anne Home,
married a Swinton, and had these children.

Notes on individuals of this surname, etc.

Robert Franche of Francheland. At Edinburgh, the 9th of
December, 1527, King James V. conceded to Johannes Marjory-
bankis in Moffet, for his service as warden of the royal tent, and
his heirs and assigns, 7 pounds 13 shillings of the lands of
Francheland, in the Stewardry of Annandie, which had been occupied by Robert Franche of Francheland.

James Franche. James Franche is among the witnesses to a
charter of Jacobus Leirmonth of Levingstoun, in favor of Gawi-
nus Hammyltoun of Drumalbane, and his heirs and assigns, of
land of Levingstoun, in the viscounty of Linlithgow, dated at

Children of the Seventh Laird.

First, Adam French, his heir who succeeded.

Second, Henry French, who evidently went to the north of Scotland very early in life; for he is found at Orkney on the 28th of October in the year 1544, and then among the many witnesses to a charter of Bishop Robert Reid to the cathedral church of Orkney, where it was dated.

Bishop Robert Reid was evidently referred to in the will of Henry French as "my lord of Orkney," from whom he "gat ane coit of Franche blak," which "he left to the abbot of Kinlos" * (who was at that time Walter Reid, a nephew of Bishop Reid), "and desirit his lordship to deliver the same to the Laird of Thornydykis, with ane velvet cap."

The name of Henry French again appears as a witness to the following charters, namely:—

Linlithgow on the 7th of October, 1535, and confirmed by the king at Striveling on the 8th of May, 1536.

James Frank. At Edinburgh, the 4th of September, 1546, Queen Mary, with consent of James, Earl of Aranie, and Lord of Hammiltoun, her tutor and gubernator, grants to James Frank, son of a certain William Frank, and his heirs and assigns, " terras Frankislandis nuncupatas " in the viscounty of Peblis, which before had been enfeoffed to the said William, but in the troublesome times he was deprived of it. Reserving for the said William 6 capita and the half-part of the infeoffment.

* The monastery of Kinloss was founded by King David I. by establishing in it a colony of his favorite Cistercians from Melrose Abbey.

First, on the 18th of September, 1550, at Edinburgh, to a charter of John Stewart of Minto to the parochial church of Aberdeen.

Second, to a charter of Patric Mowet, Lord of Boquhellie and Freschwik, wherein he makes a grant to M. Malcolmo Halcro, prebendary of the cathedral church of Orkney, dated at Elgin on the 22d of February, 1553.

Henry French appears to have acquired fishing rights on the river Spey. He died in the month of January, 1569; and by his will, given up on the 26th of January of this same year, it appears he was a brother of Adam French, the Laird of Thornydykes.

Among those named in his will were the executors of the Laird of Innes (William) and Patrick Menzeis of Abirdene; and you find Sir Andro Currie of Bassendean, James Wemis of Bowhouse, and Jonet Morray mentioned among his legatees.

" He left his saule in the handis of Almychtie God and his banes to be bureit in the muldis of Bassinden." *

---

* Bassendean was located in the southern part of Westruther, about two miles from Thornydykes. Previous to the Reformation it belonged to the nuns of Coldstream. It was most probably the burying-place of the Frenches, as it was at one time the resting-place of their neighbors, the Edgars of Wedderlie. After the Reformation Sir Andro Currie, the vicar, conveyed this place to William Home, third son of Sir John Home of Coldenknows, in Earlstone; and King James VI. gave him a charter of it on Janu. 11, 1573.

" Item the silver contenit in his purs to give thame
meit and drink that hes him to the erd." Sir Andro
Currie, the vicar of Bassendean, and Patrick French,
his brother, were both witnesses to this ancient document.

Third, Patrick French. His name appears among
the witnesses to the marriage contract of the year
1549. He is mentioned again as a witness, with his
son, James French, to a charter dated at the burgh
of Haddington, on the 31st of March, 1568, of Patrick Cockburn, prebendary of Petcokkis, belonging to
the Collegiate Church of Dunbar, wherein he grants
in gratitude and in free farm to Alexander Cockburn,
his own brother (sons of Cockburn of Langton,
county Berwick), and Alisone Vaus, his wife, one
acre of arable land in the said prebend, at Freirland,
in the western part of the territory of Dunbar, one
acre in the northern part of the prebend of Beltoun,
as well as other land, including common of pasturage
in the southern part of the village of Dunbar, in the
constabulary of Haddington, in the viscounty of Edinburgh.

Besides James French, this Patrick French appears
to have had another son, George French. He is
mentioned in the will of Henry French immediately
after Patrick French, whom he calls his brother.

A George French is found as a witness to a document dated 8th of December, 1569, in which the
contracting persons on the one part were Adam

French, eighth Laird of Thornydykes, Margaret, his wife, and James, their second son. There is another record of a George French, who is found on the 3d of September, 1576, in the service of James Sandelandis, eldar of Santmonanis.

"Patrick French is styled in the will of his brother, Adam French, as Sir Patrick French."

The three following records are found of Sir Patrick French, in relation to the vicarage of Linlithgow: —

Oct. 26, 1574. Letters purchased at the instance of Patrick Kenloche, minister at Linlithgow, against Sir Patrick Frenche, pretended titular of the vicarage of Linlithgow, and all and sundry parishioners, charging them to make payment to him of the teind sheaves for crop and year 1574.

13th of January, 1574-75. Action by Patrick Frenche, titular of the vicarage of Linlithgow, against Patrick Kenloche, minister of Linlithgow, in reference to the teinds of the said vicarage.

In the Register of the Privy Council, under the date of Nov. 13, 1587, is a Complaint of Alexander Dalmahoy of that Ilk, as follows: Sir Patrick Frensche, having been provided to the vicarage of Lynlythqu, set, during all the days of his lifetime, the same in tack to the late Mr. Andro Hereott, son of the late James Hereott of Trabroun, which tack the said Mr. Andro assigned to the complainer, so that, by virtue of the said assignation, the said complainer

has possessed the duties of the vicarage without any
question. But now he is informed that Nicoll Corn-
wall of Ballinhard, "quha is debtbound in the maist
parte of the fruitis of the said vicarage," has "movit
the said Sir Patrik to dimitt the said vicarage in his
Majesteis hands, and that, upoun the said dimissioun,
his Hienes hes presentit Patrik Kenlowy, minister
at Lynlythgow, thairto." In these circumstances the
complainer prays that the Keeper of the Privy Seal
shall be discharged from passing the said presenta-
tion till such time as the said Patrik, the presentee,
confirm the said tack and assignation thereof made
to the complainer, "and mak securitie that the said
dimissioun sall nawayes be hurtfull or prejudiciall
thairunto."

Sir Patrik Frenshe, Nicoll Cornwell, and Patrik
Kenlowy having been cited, and only the two last
appearing, while the complainer appears personally,
the Lords remit the matter to the Lords of Council
and Session, as only judges competent thereto.

Fourth, Peter French. On Nov. 13, 1552, "Queen
Mary pardons Adam French," eighth "Laird of
Thornydykes, James French,* and Peter French,
for the attacking and killing of William Halyburton
of Gogar."

---

* A James Franche was a witness at Corsby on the 4th of
September, 1556, to a charter wherein John Cranstoun grants to
his wife, Elizabeth Swyntoun, the land and barony of Bown, in
the viscounty of Berwick, and other land in the viscounty of
Edinburgh.

Peter Franche (French) was a legatee in the year 1569 of Henry Franche, in whose will he is designed as Elder, a distinction from the following legatee: " Peter Franche, my bruthir sone," evidently implying that he was the son of Peter French, " Elder."

Fifth, Hue French. About ten miles from Thornydykes, the ancestral home of the Frenches, was the Abbey of Dryburgh, which was particularly identified with the family of Erskines. Three of this name were here commendators, and probably John Erskine (who afterwards became Lord Erskine) held the same title. Hue French was in the service of this lord prior to the year 1565 (when he became Earl of Mar), during which period he had an annual income conferred upon him by John Menteith of Kers and Alwath (with the consent of Robert Menteith, his father), out of the lands and barony of Alwath, in the county of Stirling. On the 19th of December, 1567, the chamberlain of Dryburgh Abbey reports " that Hue French remained there sick after my lord's departure." Apparently, he was a pensioner of Dryburgh Abbey, as a reference is made to the pension due him for the year 1573. Soon after the coronation of King James VI. it is supposed by the influence of his patron, John Erskine, now Earl of Mar, that he entered the royal service as " Controller of his majesties Horse"; and it is most probable that he held this position at the time of his decease, for at that time he was still in the service of King James.

. Hue French died in the month of October of the
year 1574; and his will appears to have been given
up on the 25th of the preceding month, in the house
of John Gillespy, within the burgh of Stirling, in the
presence of John Gillespy, John Wilson, Patrick
Bauchap, and John French, his brother's son. It
confirms the royal patronage, refers to some nephews,
nieces, and a half brother and sister. By this will he
appoints Christopher Murray, Constable of Stirling
Castle, and Adam French, Laird of Thornydykes, as
his executors.

Sixth, Alexander French, who appears as a witness,
on July 2, 1567, to several tacks by John Lermonth,
vicar of the parish church of Gogar, of the diocese of
St. Andrews.

He is mentioned in the year 1569 as one of the executors of his brother Henry French, and is found
again as a witness as late as the year 1573.

Seventh, Robert French, who is called in the year
1569 brother german of Henry French, and is supposed to have been the minister who lived at this time
in Berwickshire. There is a record of him at Eccles
in 1567, at Lammas in 1571; and after the death of
Sir Andrew Turnbull (of the Bedrule family) the vicar
of Greenlaw, King James conferred upon him on
April 23, 1573, that vicarage. In the Acts and Decreets of the 6th of July of this same year were "Letters purchased at the instance of Robert Frenche
against Alexander Brounfield in Eastfield and Ninian

Brounfield, and all others the parishioners of the
vicarage of Greenlaw, lying within the diocese of
St. Andrews and sheriffdom of Berwick, for payment
of the fruits and teinds thereof, the collection of
the same having been gifted by the king to the
said Robert. Decerned against the said defenders."
He was translated to Home about 1574, when Stit-
chell, Gordon, Eccles, and Greenlaw were also in his
charge. He is mentioned of Eccles on the 12th of
September, 1577, and again in 1583. In 1589–90 he
with David Hume and Johanne Clappertoun were
the ecclesiastical commissioners appointed for the
shire of Berwick to put an act of Parliament in force
against the Jesuits. Legerwood was conferred upon
him by the king on May 18, 1592. He returns to
Eccles in 1596, where he appears as late as 1601.

There is a record of a John French at Eccles in
1599, who may have been his son.

Eighth, Jonet French, who is mentioned in the wills
of her brothers Henry and Hue French. She married first Robert Watson of Yiflie, in Westruther,
county Berwick, who appears to have died before
February 5, 1546. He left a son of the same name,
to whom his uncle Henry French refers as his sister's
son.

The record of the year 1546 shows "that she was
then married to Robert Cranstoun of Broxmouth," in
the parish of Dunbar, in Haddingtonshire.

On Sept. 25, 1550, Janet French renounces her

right of conquest and life rent of the third part of the lands of Iverlie, in the parish of Westruther, in favor of her son Robert Watson.

Jonet French is mentioned as late as the year 1574.

Ninth, Margaret French, who married first George Nesbit of Raclewcht (near Thornydykes).

The following is the agreement for the marriage :—

The auchtene day of May, in the yeir of God J^m V^c fourty and nyne yeris, it is appoyntit aggreit contrakkit and finalie endit betuix thir honourable men and parteis, that ar to say Alexander Franche, Johnne Franche, brethir to vmquhile Robert Franche, lard of Thorniedikis, Robert Rankyn, Johnne Pacok, Johne Boyd, Archibald Burnle, Johnne Bell, and Margreit Franche on that ane part, and George Nesbit in the Raclewcht on that vther part, that the said George Nesbit godwilland sall compleit and fulfill the haly band of matrimony with the said Margreit Franche, in maner effect and forme as efter followis : That is for to say the saidis Alexander Franche and Johne Franche for thair partis of the completing of the said band of matrimony betuix the saidis George Nesbit and the said Margreit Franche bindis and oblissis thame thair airis executouris and assignayis conjunctlie and severalie, be the fathis and trewthis of thair bodeis and be the tennour of this present writting bindis thame for to content and pay the sowm of ane hundreth pundis of gud and vsuale

money of this realme of Scotland, and the saidis
sowmes of money to be payit betuix the dait of this
present contract and obligatioun and the feist of
Sanct androis day nixtocum; and Robert Rankyne,
Johnne Pacok, Johnne Boyd, Archibald Brunle, and
Johnne Bell for thair partis bindis and oblissis thame
as said is conjunctlie and severalie ane as all and all
as ane thair airis executouris and assignais for to content and pay the sowm of ane hundreth merkis of gud
and vsuale money of Scotland.   And the said sowm
to be payit within five yeris nixt efter the dait of this
present contract, and attour we the saidis Alexander
Franche, Johnne Franche, Robert Rankyn, Johnne
Pacok, Johne Boyd, Archibald Brunlie, and Johnne
Bell, we bind ws as said is for to fulfill content and
pay the sowmes abonewrittin in and to the said
George Nesbit his airis, executouris, and assignais, at
the dayis and termes abonewrittin, and attour for the
mair securite that the said contract salbe registrat in
the bukis of counsale on the said George Nesbittis
expenssis, within xv dais nixt efter the dait of this
present contract and obligatioun, and attour this
beand done ather of the saidis parteis bindis thame
that the said band of matrimony within xv dais
salbe compleittit and fulfillit or ellis the party brek-
and sall content and pay to the party kepand the
sowm of five hundreth merkis gud and vsuale money
of Scotland, the quhilk sowm salbe payit within the
space of ane yeir nixt efter the dait heirof, and attour

in tyme to cum gif thair movis ony mater twiching
ony consanguinite or affinite of blud the party
movand the samyn sall bring hame gif neid beis dis-
pensatioun or dispensations on their awin expenssis
and forder all thir parteis abonewrittin bindis thame
as said is to fulfill all the poyntis and artikillis of the
said contract, and for the mair securite and verifica-
tioun of the samyn we haif subscrivit this our present
contract and obligatioun with our handis at the pen
the said day, tyme, and place abonewrittin befoir thir
witnesses Johnne Hume of Blacater, Adam Franche
of Thornydikis, Thomas Hume, Johnne Hoppringill,
and Patrik Franche with vtheris divers.   Sic subscribitur.

> Alex^r Franche w^t my hand at ye pen.
> Johnne Franche w^t my hand at ye pen.
> Robene Rankyn w^t my hand at ye pen.
> Johne Pacok w^t my hand at ye pen.
> Johne Boyd w^t my hand at ye pen.
> Archibald Burnle w^t my hand at ye pen.
> Johnne Bell w^t my hand at ye pen.

Ita est Robertus Lyell presbyter eiusdem diocesis
ac notarius publicus omnibus et singulis premissis.

George Nesbit of (Nether) Racleuch, died before
Dec. 1, 1564, at which date Margaret French, his
wife, is mentioned, as well as their sons John and
George Nesbit.

The second husband of Margaret French was another George Nesbit, as appears by a record as early as the 22d of March, 1566–67.

John Nesbit, the son of Margaret, is mentioned the 26th of November, 1567.

Under date of the 21st of June, 1576, may be found the name of John Nesbit, Margaret French, his mother, and George Nesbit, spouse to the said Margaret.

Margaret French is again recorded on the 27th of May, 1583, as well as her son, Robert Nesbit.

Tenth, Elspeth French, who is mentioned as a legatee, in the year 1574, in the will of her brother, Hue French.

EIGHTH LAIRD OF THORNYDYKES.

Adam French, eighth Laird of Thornydykes, the eldest son, was a minor on the death of his father. John French, his uncle, had the gift of the relief of the estates, as well as that of his marriage. He succeeded to his inheritance before April, 1549. On the 18th of May of that year he is mentioned as Adam French of Thornydykes, and again on the 13th of November, 1552. On the 9th of December, 1552, the Register of Acts and Decreets shows that he was summoned in an action as the son and heir of his deceased father, Robert French. On the 8th of February, 1555–56, Queen Mary grants a charter to Adam Franche of Thornydikes, and Margaret Hoppringill, his spouse, of the lands of Thornydikes, with manor place, mills, etc., in Berwickshire, and of a tenandry of the land in the toun of Petcokkis, in the constabulary of Haddington, on the resignation

---

NOTE. On the 8th of January, 1556, a William Franche is mentioned as occupier of a cottage and land in Whittinghane, Haddingtonshire.

Christall Frenche is witness to a charter to Andrew Ker of Hirsell, of the lands of Lessuden, dated at Dryburgh Abbey, 10th of April, 1567.

thereof by the said Adam, personally, in the hands of
the queen.

Abstract of a contract dated at Edinburgh, 27th of
August, 1563, between "Johnne Home of Coldane-
knawis and Williame Home, his sone, portionar of
Kelso, and the said Johnne Home acting for his son,"
on the one part, "and Adame Franche in Thornedykis, David Spottiswod of that ilk, Henry Wod in
Flas, Johne Wod in Flas, and Johnne Alexander in
Hekspeth," on the other part. "That is to say, fforsamekill as the said Williame Home, portioner foirsaid hawand assignit to him the bollis of meill vnder-
written for the teind schewis of the landis vnderspeci-
feit liand within the parochin of Gordoun in part of
payment of his said pentioun quhilk he hes of the
said Abbace of Kelso," "the said Johnne Home of
Coldinknowis, Williame, his sone, and the said lard
takand the burding vpoun him for his said sone, hes
sauld assignit and disponit lik as thai be the tennour
heirof sellis assignis and disponis the foirsaid bollis
respective as followis : —

"That is to say the said Adame Frenche of
Thornedykis, his said xviij bollis meill quhilk suld
be payit for his teindis of his saidis landis of Thornedykis, and to the said David Spottiswod of that ilk
his said ten bollis meill quhilk suld be payit yeirlie
for the teindis of his landis of Spottiswod, to the
said Henry Wod four bollis of meill quhilk suld be
payit yeirlie for his teindis of Ywelie, and sewin fur-

lettis meill for the teindis of the said Henryis part
of the wast syd of the Flas, and to the said Johnne
Wod sewin furlettis meill quhilk suld be payit for his
part of the wast syd of the Flas, and to the said
Johnne Alexander four bollis meill quhilk suld be
payit for the half of Hekspeth yeirlie and ilk yeirlie
sa lang as the said Williame Home hes rycht to the
saidis teindis and to vptak the same."

"The said Johnne Home and Williame, his sone,
bindis and oblissis thame and thair airis to warrand
acquiet and defend the foirsaidis personis and thair
airis of all the meill and prices thairof quhilk thai
sal happin to ressave fra thame for thair teindis of all
yeiris be vertew of this contract."

Witnessed by Maister Johnne Abircrummy, advo-
cat; Johnne Edzer of Wadderle; Alexander Banner-
feild; Johne Young, writter; and Williame McCart-
nay, notar, with vtheris divers.

Among the contemporaries of Adam French, in
Berwickshire, in the year 1565, were the following
persons : —

> John Home of Blacater.
> David Home of Wedderburn.
> John Lumisden of Blanerne.
> George Home of Ayton.
> Patrick Cockburn of Langtone.
> John Swinton of that Ilk.
> Alexander Cockburn of that Ilk.
> John Rantoune of Billie.

Pat. Lleigh of Cumledge.
William Chyrnside of East Nesbitt.
John Sinclair of Longformacus
Thomas Ridpath of that Ilk.
John Haitlie of Mellerstaines.
James Ker of Mersington.

17th of July, 1567. Action by Adam Fransche of Thornydykes, against Margaret Hepburn and George Haliburtoun of Over Gogar, her spouse; Archibald and James Hoppringle, sons to the said Margaret; and William Hepburn, tutor and curator to the said Archibald; and Henry Frude, pretended occupier and tenant of the lands of Petcokkis belonging to the pursuer, who had warned them to remove therefrom, but they had refused. The lords now ordain them to flit and remove from said lands.

NOTE. 1567, April 26. Charter of Robert Stewart of Orcadia, then perpetual commendator of Saint Crux, in which it convenants and grants, in gratitude and in free farm, to John Frenche, his servant, the inheritance of a garden with a house in the same (newly built and taken in possession by the said John), situated in the northern boundary of the monastic cemetery (near the way to the monastery, the village of Leith, the royal garden, and land occupied by David Levingstoun). Besides, he receives another garden (formerly occupied by George Hannay) in the regality and barony of Brochtoun, in the viscounty of Edinburgh. Reserving annually for the monastery 3 shillings, 4 pennies, with actual sasine to John Logane. Witnesses, M. Alexander Chalmer, chamberlain of the said monastery, Magister David Makgill, William Pennycuik, the rector of the monastery, Thoma Robesoun, servant of the commendator.

21st of November, 1567. Margaret Hepburn and Geo. Haliburton, her spouse, against Adam Franche of Thornydykes, for suspension and summons of removing the suspenders, having found caution that they should remove from Petcokkys.

6th of December, 1567. Adam Fransche of Thornydykes, against Stevin Bourhill, Alexander Fairbairn, John Broune, John Burnett, James Michill, and others, pretended tenants of the pursuer's lands of Fawnes, Langriggs, and Thornydykes in the shire of Berwick, to remove therefrom. The lords decern accordingly.

Octavo Decembris, anno Domini J^m V^c lxix^o In presens of the lordis of counsale comperit personalie Andro commendator of Jedburgh, and Matho Home of Rowchlaw, and Jhone Couser, burges of Edinburgh, as cautioneris and sverteis for him on that ane part, and Adam Frenche of Thornedikis for him self and Margaret Hoppringle, his spous, on that vther part, and gaif in this contract and appunctnament vnderwrittin subscrivit with thair handis and desyrit the samin to be insert and registrat in the bukis of counsale, to haif the strenth, force, and effect of thair act and decreit in tyme tocum, and lettres and executorialis to be direct apoun ayther of thame partis and souerteis foirsaidis for fulfilling thairof in all pointis in maner specifeit thairintill. The quhilk desyre the saidis lordis thocht ressonable, and thair-

foir hes ordanit and ordanis the said contract and
appunctnament to be insert and registrat in the
saidis bukis, to haif the strenth, force, and effect of
thair act and decreit in tyme tocum, and hes inter-
ponit and interponis their auctorite thairto, and
decernis and ordanis lettrez and executorialis to be
direct vpoun ather of the saidis partiis and thair
souerteis for fulfilling thairof in all pointis in maner
specifeit thairintill in form as efferis off the quhilk
the tenour followis: At Edinburgh, the sevint day
of December, the yeir of God J^m V^c lxix yeiris. It is
appunctit aggreit and finalie concludit betuix thir
honourable personis: To wit, ane venerable man,
Andro Commendator of the abbay of Jedburgh,
fewer of the landis vnderwrittin on that ane part,
and Adam Franche of Thornidikis, Margaret Hoppryngle, his spous, and James Frenche, thair secund
sone, on the vthair part in maner following: that is
to say, fforsamekill as the said commendator be thir
presentis grantis hym selff to haif ressavit fra the
said Adame and his said spous partlie at this present
tyme and of befoir the sowme of threttie hundryth
merkis vsuale money of this realme quhairof he
haldis hym weill content satisfyit and payit and
exoneris quytclames and dischargeis the said Adame
and his said spous thair airis executouris and assignayis thairof for ever be thir presentis. Thairfoir the
said commendator bindis and oblissis hym and his
airis to mak seill subscrive and delyver ane sufficient

chartour and precept of sesing of alienatioun titulo
oneroso maid be hym to the said Adame and his said
spous the langer levir of thame twa in lyferent for all
the dayis of thair lyfetyme and to the said James
thair secund sone his airis and assignayis quhatsumever heretable of all and haill ane annuelrent of sevin
score merkis and sextene vsuale money of this realme
yeirlie to be vpliftit at twa termeis in the yeir Witsoneday and Mertiemess in wynter be equall por-
sionis of all and syndre the said commendatoris few
landis vnderwrittin or ony part thairof. To witt of
all and haill the toun and landis of Vlstoun over
manis of Vlstoun the landis of Greithillis Pryour
medowis Chepmansyde with the wod of the samin
the landis of Spettelstanis the thre husband landis
in Nethir Craling Togidder with half ane husband
land in Over Nisbeth ane husband land in Nethir
Nysbeth the landis of Plowlandis the landis of Fyn-
lawis callit Newhall the landis of Haucheid and land
in Cesfurdburyne the landis of Justicielie with the
teyndis thairof the landis of Auld Jedburgh and
landis of Rowcastell ane pece land in Langnewtoun
the landis and toun of Abbotisrewle and landis
of Bowatsyde the landis of Grange with the mylne
of the samin the landis of Foderly the landis of
over Bunchester nethir Bunchester with the woddis
of the samin the landis of Maxsyde the landis of
Gathouscott with the woddis of the samin the landis
of Hartishauch the landis of Langraw with the

teyndis thairof the landis and toun of Rapperlaw the
landis of Firth with the teyndis and woddis of the
samin the landis of Westbarnis with the teyndis
thairof the landis callit the Brewlandis in Rapperlaw
the landis of Belcheis with the mylne of the samin
the landis and toun of over Ancrum with the mylne
and coittageis thairof the landis of Henhousfeild the
landis of Castelwod and Castelhill with the woddis
of the samin Togidder with the aikeris lyand besyde
the Freiris of Jedburgh and the Kirklandis of Spittell callit crucur Spittell and manor place thairof
with mylnis teyndis and all vtheris thair pertinentis
lyand within the Sherefdome of Roxburgh All and
haill the tenement of land bak and foir with the pertinentis lyand within the burgh of Jedburgh on the
south syde of the Kingis streit thairof in the barronie
of Vlstoun within the Sherefdome of Roxburgh betuix
the tenement of umquhile James Ryddell and now
of Robert Rutherfurd on the south the wattcr of Jedburgh on the west syde the clos of the said abbacie
on the eist and the Kingis streit of the said burgh
on the north To be haldin of the said commendator
his airis and assignayis in fre blensche heretable and
in lyferent as said is for payment yeirlie of ane
pennie in name of blensche ferme gif it be askit with
sufficient claus of warrandice contenit thairintill
oblissand the said commendator his airis and assignayis to warand acquyet and defend the foirsaid
annuelrent fre fra all wardis nonentress releifis for-

faltouris recognitionis purprusionis alienationis con-
junctfeis ladyis terceis takis or vtheris inconvenientis
or perrellis quhatsumever bigane and to cum in the
maist sure forme as may be devysit be the law and
this infeftment to be maid seillit subscrivit and dely-
verit as said is with all diligence ffor the quhilk caus
the said Adame his said spous and James thair sone
sall mak seill subscrive and delyver to the said commendator ane sufficient Lettre of Reversioun maid
be thame to hym his airis and assignayis contenand
the said sowme of xiij^c merkis as said is for redemptioun of the said annuelrent to be payit in the
nethir Tolbuyth of Edinburgh vpone fourtie dayis
wairning as vse is with this provisioun to be contenit
thairintill That it sall nocht be leissum to the said
commendator his airis and assignayis to redeme the
said annuelrent be payment of the said sowme for
the space of thre yeiris nixt eftir the dait heirof and
that all byrun annuellis be fullelie payit with the
said principale sowme at the redemptioun thairof
befoir the samin be grantit lauchfulle redemit And
for the sure payment of the said annuelrent yeirlie
and termelie quhill the lauchfull redemptioun thairof
as said is the said commendator and Matho Home of
Rochlow and Johne Cosser burges of Edinburgh as
souerteis for hym be thir presentis bindis and oblissis
thame conjunctle and severale thair airis executouris
and assignayis to content pay and thankfulle delyvir
to the saidis Adame his spous the langer levir of

thame twa and to the said James his airis and assignayis the foirsaid annuelrent of sevin score xvj
merkis money foirsaid at the termes abonewrittin
unto the lauchfull redemptioun thairof begynnand
the first termeis payment of the samin at the feist
of Witsoneday nixttocum and the saidis commendator and Matho oblissis thame conjunctlie and
severalie thair airis executouris and assignayis to
releif and keip skaythles the said Johne Cosser his
airis executouris and assignayis of the premissis at
the handis of the saidis personis abonewrittin And
for the mair securite heirof the said parteis and
souerteis foirsaidis ar content and consentis that this
present contract be actit and registrat in the buikis
of our soverane lordis counsale and decernit to haif
the strenth of ane decreit thairof with executoriallis
of hoirnyng or poynding to be direct thairupone in
forme as effeiris And to that effect makis constitutis
and ordanis Maister Johne Abircrumby and ilkane
of thame conjunctle and severalie thair verray lauchfull and undowtit procuratouris committand power to
thame to compeir befoir the lordis of counsale quhatsumever day or dayis place or placeis lauchfull and
to consent to the registring of thir presentis pro-
mittentes de rato In witnes heirof the saidis parteis
hes subscrivit this present contract with thair handis
as efter followis day yeir and place foirsaidis Befoir
thir witnes George Cranstoun of Corsbie, Alexander
Carstairis, Barnard Haitlie, Thomas Trotter, George

Frenche and Maister Williame Broun with vthairis divers sic subscribitur.

Andro Commendator of Jedbur{ }^t.

Adame Frensche of Thornydykis w{ }^t my hand.

Matho Home of Rowchlaw.

Johne Cosser w{ }^t my hand.

Margarett Hoppryngle abonewrittin with my hand at the pen led be the notar underwrittin.

Ita est Magister Georgius Freir notarius publicus manu propria.

February 4, 1574–75. Action at the instance of William Hume, son to the deceased John Hume of Coldounknowis, knight, against Adam Frenche of Thorniedykis, Ninian Spottiswod of that Ilk, son and heir of the deceased David Spottiswod of that Ilk, Henry Wod of Flas, John Wod there, and John Alexander, in Espeth, touching the spoliation of and intromitting with the teind-sheaves of their lands lying within the parish of Gordoun and sheriffdom of Berwick. Continued till 12th of March next.

The will of Adam French is mentioned as being dated at Thornydyke Castle on the 3d of October, 1570.

In the Register of Acts and Decreets reference is made to "a contract between John Baillie and Adam French, dated the 1st of April, 1576," so that Adam French must have died soon after this date, as his will is stated to have been recorded in February,

1578, and Margaret Hoppringle is called relict of Adam French on the following 16th of December.

Under the date of the 23d of February, 1582–83, is an action at the instance of Margaret Hoppringill, relict of Adam Frenche of Thornedykis, and Robert ——, son and apparent heir of the said deceased Adam, and executors testamentars confirmed to him, against Cuthbert Cranstoun of Thirlstanemains, Thomas Cranstoun, in Rymmiltoun, his son, William Nesbit in Bellielaw, George Young in Ledgirtwod, and Robert Scot in Rymmiltounlaw, for the violent spoliation from the lands of Jordanhill, mains of Thornydykis and Langriggis, lying in the sheriffdom of Berwick, pertaining to the pursuers, in 1569 and 1573 of diverse oxen, kye, horses, sheep, goods, and gear.

23d of February, 1582–83. Action at the instance of Margaret Hoppringill, relict of Adam Frenche of Thornydykis, cessioner and assignee donatrix in and to the ward lands of the mains of East Gordoun and mill of the same, lying in the sheriffdom of Berwick, against Cuthbert Cranstoun of Thirlstanemains, Thomas Cranstoun in Rimmiltounlaw, his son, Patrick Hallyday in Farnyngtoun, William Schort in Bellielaw, George Johnstoun in East Gordoun, Thomas Aymeir there, George Broun there, and William Millar in Bow, for the violent ejection of the said Margaret and servants out of the said lands and mains of

East Gordoun, mill thereof, and Bowhouse in September, 1581.

"Lady Margaret Hoppringill, Lady Thornydykis, relict of vmquhile Adame Frensche of Thornydykis within the scheriffdome of Beruik," her brother was Robert Hoppringill, and she was the daughter of the Laird of Blindlie,* in Selkirkshire, a descendant from John, whose father was James Hoppringle or Pringle of Smailholme and Galashields. She died March 21, 1582. It seems quite evident, that Margaret Hoppringle was a widow French at the time she married Adam French; for in her will, before mentioning any of their children, she specially makes the following bequests to "hir dochters Bessie and Katherine Frensche": "Item thair wes awand be the said vmquhle Margaret Hoppringill, Lady Thornedykis, to Alexander Cauldcleuch in Horsupcleuch for the rest of tocher gude promittit be the defunct to him with Bessie Frensche, hir dochter, the soum of Twa hundreth lxxx merkis. Item to Alexander Carrik in Northberuik for the rest of his tocher gude promottit be the defunct with Katherine Frensche, hir dochter, the soume of twa hundreth and fiftie merkis."

In this will she mentions "James Frensche, my secund sone, my onelie executour," "Robert Hoppringill of Blindlie, bruther germane, and Johne Dicksoun of Belchester" "lauchfull administratouris tutouris

---

* Blindlie was near Galashields. As late as 1878, it was spoken of as "Blindlie Birks," but more commonly as "The Birks."

gydaris and governouris" of certain children. Further, the aforesaid Margaret, Lady Thornydykis, "or-
dinis Andro" (Home), "Commendatar of Jedburgh,
ouirisman to the saidis haill barnes and to se the
equall destributioun of the gudis and geir abonemen-
tionat amangis thame and that na thing be done be
the saidis James Frensche executour foirsaid Robert
Hoppringill and Johne Diksoun without the speciall
licence and assent of the said Andro Commendatar
of Jedburgh had obtenit thairto Attoure I the said
Margaret levis and disponis my haill wering clathis
to be devidit and pairtit equalie betuix Margaret and
Cristiane Frensches alanerlie and siclyk levis and
disponis the haill plennesing and insycht to be
equalie and proportionalie devidit and pairtit betuix
the said James, Johne, Alexander, Margaret, and
Cristiane Frensches, and that at the sicht and discre-
tioun of the said Andro Commendatar of Jedburgh,
Robert Hoppringill of Blindlie, and Johne Diksoun
of Belchester ouerismen foirsaidis."

Children of the Eighth Laird.

First, Robert French, who succeeded.

Second, James French. He is mentioned in 1569
as the second son, and Hue French calls him in the
year 1574 his nephew. He was appointed by his
mother in 1582 as executor to her will. In 1583 he
instituted proceedings against Andrew Home, abbot

of Jedburgh, and died *s.p.* soon after his brother
Robert.

Third, John French. He was a nephew of Hue
French, who was " Controller of Horse " for King
James VI. On the 25th of September, 1574, he was
present at Stirling at the making and giving up of
this uncle's will. His name is mentioned again by
his mother on the 19th of March, 1582 ; and possibly
he may have been the Royal Palefrenier of this name
who had the grants of escheats. One of these gifts
of the crown came as late as the year 1588–89.

After the decease of his brother James he became
tutor of Thornydykes. In 1598 William Lauder, the
royal bailiff of the burgh of Lauder, called Williame
of the West Port, in the king's residence of Lanark
was attacked and killed, and the royal residence
burnt by a party consisting of Alexander, Earl of
Home; Lord John Home of Huttone Hall, knight;
Master Samuel Home, his brother; Thomas Tyrie,
tutor of Drumkilbo; Alexander and John Frenches,
brothers of Robert French of Thornydykis; Joh
Home, in Kello; Robert Home, in Huttone; Robert
Auchincraw, servant of the said earl of Home; John
Cranstoun, son of John Cranstoun of Morestoun;
Ninian Chirnesyde, servant of the said earl; Walter
Trumble of Ramflat; Robert Home, son of William
Home of Aytoun; William, Ninian, and Archibald
Homes, sons of the late William Home of St. Leon-
ardis; and John Carutheris. But on the 17th of

November, 1607, King James pardons and forgives
them all for those crimes and offences.

He was served heir of his brother James on April
4, 1605, and on May 6 of the same year was one
of the jury on the service of Thomas Cranstoun of
Morristoun, in county Berwick. He died between
the years 1609 and 1612.

Fourth, Alexander French. He succeeded as tutor
or guardian of Thornidykes on the death of his
brother John. He was a turbulent character, mixed
up with the political troubles of the Earl of Bothwell,
and committed other lawless acts, and finally came to
an untimely end on March 13, 1612.

One of his sisters appears to have married ——
Wicht ——, and had a son, James Wicht.

Fifth, Thomas French. He is mentioned as early
as the year 1574. If judged by the many escheats
and other marks of royal favours conferred upon him
over a series of years, they would indicate he was a
favorite with his sovereign. On Nov. 4, 1595, he was
appointed to the "office of only keeper of his majesty's outher chamber door," with a yearly salary and
allowance for his livery, which position he appears to
have held for many years. He was in the king's service in 1599, and a pension was granted him on November 22d of that year out of the lands of Hirsell, in
Berwickshire. He is recorded servitor of his majesty
on March 6, 1600, and is mentioned on the 19th of
September of the following year as the usher of his

majesty's outer chamber. There is a record of his being in royal service in 1604, and on the 18th of April of that year Alexander Livingston of Donypace calls him his "guid freind."

Sixth, Margaret French, who is named in the will of her mother, Lady Thornydykes.

Seventh, Christiane French, who is also mentioned in the will of her mother. Her name is also found on the 11th of January, 1593, in the will of Margaret Trumbell, the first wife of Robert French, ninth Laird of Thornydykes, her brother.

Eighth, Jonet French, who is referred to on the 25th of September, 1574, in the will of her uncle, Hue French.

Ninth, Euphan French, who is named by some writers as being another daughter.

Robert French, the *ninth Laird of Thornydykes*, succeeded his father, Adam French, and is stated to have entered heir after the death of his mother in 1583. He is referred to in the will of his uncle, Hue French, who died in 1574, and mentioned again as the son of the late Adam French on the 16th of December, 1578. He is called Robert French of Thornydykes, on Nov. 13, 1587; and in the will of his mother, Margaret Hoppringill, who died the 21st of March, 1582, she refers to him as her eldest son. "He was juror on the service of Robert Lauder of that Ilk, on the 7th of April, 1584." A feud sprang up between the Spottiswoods and Frenches, which resulted in the death of Ninian Spottiswood of that Ilk, on the 15th of November, 1588, for which Robert French of Thornydykes, James French and John French, his brothers, and Robert Quhippo, his servant, obtained a respite on the 19th of February, 1594-95.

This time was a period of much trouble in Scotland. The conditions of affairs were described by King James when "he professes to be scandalised at

the state of the commonweal altogether disorderit
and shaken louss by reason of the deidly feids and
controversies standing amongs his subjects of all de-
grees, and in order to help matters the Privy Council
ordainit letters to be sent charging the various parties
to make their appearance before the king on certain
days, each accompanied with a certain number of
friends who might assist with their advice, but the
whole party in each case to keep their lodging after
their coming, till they be specially sent for by his
majesty." According to these regulations of the 23d
of December, 1595, among the letters ordered to be
sent by the Privy Council were those to John, Earl
of Montrose, and Robert French of Thornydykes,
the latter being allowed 24 persons as his retinue.

Robert French died in 1603, and appears to have
been the last tenant of the king of the direct line of
the Frenches of Thornydykes.

He married prior to the 14th of June, 1589, as his
first wife, Margaret, only daughter and heiress of the
late William Turnbull, Lord of Bedreule, in the viscounty of Roxburgh. Her mother was Margaret,
daughter of Sir John Home of Coldenknowes; and
her uncle was James Home of Coldenknowes. She
died the 20th of June, 1593. In her will of the 11th
of June of the same year it is found that her executors were " Robert Frensche of Thornidykis, hir
spous, Williame Home in Bassindene, and Mr.
Thomas Cranstoun of Morestoun." She refers also

to " my sone, his appeirand air," who must have soon after died, and makes bequests to " Alexander, Thomas, Barbara, Elizabethe, Agnes, and Issobell Cranstounes sones and dochteris lauchfull to the aforesaid Mr. Thomas Cranstoun."

The second wife of Robert French was Margaret, daughter of Mark Home of Hardiesmylne, and sister of William Home, of the same place.

His wife survived him, as appears by a record of the 7th of February, 1605 ; and by this marriage he had all his surviving children.

Children of the Ninth Laird.

First, Adam French, his heir.

Second, Jean French, who married John Cranston, brother of William, Lord Cranston, and succeeded with her sisters as heirs portioners of her father and her brother.

Third, Alison French, who married, first, Thomas Cranston of Huntliewood, and, second, William Marjoribanks of Stainerig.

Fourth, Margaret French, who married Robert Brownfield of Totrig, county Berwick.

Adam French, tenth Laird of Thornydykes, son of Robert French, the ninth Laird, and Margaret Home, was born in the year 1599, and was baptized on the 12th of November, 1601. On the death of his father in 1603, being a minor, he became a ward of the crown. His uncle, James, not being able to discharge the administration of his nephew's affairs, made choice of their mutual friend and kinsman, Sir Johnne Home of North Berwick; and " King James VI. on the 3d of October, 1603, presented Sir John Home of North Berwick, with the gift of the ward and nonentry duties of the lands of Thornydikes, manor place, houses, etc., and of the lands of Petcoks, since the death of Robert Frenche of Thornydykes, and until the entry of the rightful heir, with the gift of the marriage of Adam Frensche, son and apparent heir to the said Robert." It appears, however, that Sir John Home held only nominally the position of donator; but the active duties were performed by James French until his decease, when he was succeeded by his brother, John French. After his demise Sir John Home assumed the active duties of donator, as we ascertain by his sending Adam French to the school at Haddington, to be placed under the charge of William Bowrie, the schoolmaster of that place. At the time of the forcible abduction and marriage of Adam French, William Home of Hardiesmylne, his uncle on the maternal side, took him away from the house of William Bowrie, with the plausible excuse of visiting Margaret Haitlie, his "guidame and sisteris," but with the real intention of marrying him, and that without the consent of Sir John Home, the donator to the gift of his ward and marriage. From Haddington this uncle carried him to Rymmeltonelaw in the Merse, the dwelling-house of Alexander Cranstoun of Moristoun. From thence he was conveyed, by William Home, Alexander Cranstoun, John Cranstoun, brother of William Lord Cranstoun, and William Moffet, to the place of East Nesbit, and therefrom out of the realm of Scotland to the town of Berwick, in England, where he was secretly married, on Nov. 16, 1615, to Jean, daughter of Sir Patrick Chirnesyde of East Nisbet. In consequence of this abduction and marriage a trial ensued on Nov. 8, 1616, of which Pitcairn gives a long account. The parties interested were required to keep the peace under heavy penalties, and the marriage of Adam French to Jean Chirnesyde was eventually gifted by the king; but there was no issue by it, and the young husband died in wardship in

February, 1617, which brought to an end the ancient direct male line of the Frenches of Thornydykes.

Soon after the demise of Adam French it appears that the estates of Thornydyke and Petcoke reverted to the crown because of feudal delinquency, of which we have the following explanation from the Registry of the Great Seal : —

" The estates of Thornydyke and Petcoke belonged of inheritance to Jane, Alice, and Margaret French, daughters and heirs in common of the late Robert Frenche of Thornydyke, or to the late Adam French, their brother, or to the said the late Robert French, their father, or to the late —— French of ——, their grandfather, or to the late —— Frenche of ——, their great-grandfather, or to certain other of their ancestors, by them or some one or more of them held directly from us and our illustrious progenitors per servitium warde et relevii [a feudal tenure] and now belong to us and have fallen and come into our hands and within our disposition by the privilege of our crown and under the laws, and after the custom and practice of the said Kingdom of Scotland, because of the alienation and disposition made by the aforesaid Jane, Alice, and Margaret French, and by the said their late brother, father, grandfather, great-grandfather, or any other of their ancestors whomsoever to whatever person or persons of the lands, and other property aforesaid with their appurtenances or of the largest part thereof, or of the annual income of

said lands and other property aforesaid with the appurtenances annually to be accrued."

"Which lands and the annual income thereof,
alienated and disposed of as is permitted, exceed the
largest part of the annual rent, profit, and produce of
the lands and other property respectively specified
above with their appurtenances, and this without our
consent, permission, or approval, or that of our predecessors first before had and obtained."

"Wherefore, all and singular the estates and other
property aforesaid with their appurtenances now belong to us, and have fallen and come into our hands
by reason of the recognizance as aforesaid."

The estates of Thornydyke and Petcoke remained
in the hands of the crown until the 26th of January,
1619, when they were given by a charter of King
James to Adam Frenche of Frenchland, in Dumfries-
shire, a very distant kinsman of Jeane, Alice, and
Margaret French, the pedigree of his family showing
he was a descendant of Robert French, third Laird
of Thornydyke, who died some time prior to the year
1478. This Adam French of Frenchland did not
long retain possession of the estates; for in the year
1633 he conveyed them to George Brown (the second
son of the Laird of Colston), who is afterwards
called the Laird of Thornydyke, and the Frenches of
Frenchland thereafter only designed themselves as
lineal representatives of the Frenches of Thornydyke.